At ✳ Issue

The Right to Die

John Woodward, *Book Editor*

Bruce Glassman, *Vice President*
Bonnie Szumski, *Publisher*
Helen Cothran, *Managing Editor*

GREENHAVEN PRESS
An imprint of Thomson Gale, a part of The Thomson Corporation

THOMSON
GALE

Detroit • New York • San Francisco • San Diego • New Haven, Conn.
Waterville, Maine • London • Munich

For more information, contact
Greenhaven Press
27500 Drake Rd.
Farmington Hills, MI 48331-3535
Or you can visit our Internet site at http://www.gale.com

LIBRARY OF CONGRESS CATALOGING-IN-PUBLICATION DATA

The right to die / John Woodward, book editor.
   p. cm. — (At issue)
Includes bibliographical references and index.
ISBN 0-7377-3440-X (pbk. : alk. paper) — ISBN 0-7377-3439-6 (lib. : alk. paper)
   1. Right to die—Law and legislation—United States. 2. Euthanasia—Law and legislation—United States. I. Woodward, John, 1958– . II. At issue (San Diego, Calif.)
KF3827.E87R58 2006
344.7304'197—dc22
                                                      2005050522

Printed in the United States of America

Contents

Introduction

On March 25, 2005, ten-year-old Gabriel Keys was arrested at a Florida hospice for trying to bring a glass of water to a person unable to eat or drink on her own. His fourteen-year-old sister Josie, twelve-year-old brother Cameron, and his father, Chris, were also arrested. The object of their sympathy, Terri Schiavo, was slowly dying. The fate of Schiavo touched far more people than the Keys; indeed, it ignited a national controversy.

Twenty-six-year-old Terri Schiavo suffered a heart attack on February 25, 1990, which doctors believe was brought on by a bulimia-induced potassium deficiency. The lack of oxygen while her heart was stopped caused brain damage, and doctors diagnosed her as being in a persistent vegetative state. Unable to eat or drink on her own, she was kept alive with a feeding tube. Her husband, Michael, testified in court that Terri had once told him that she would not want to be kept alive by artificial means, which is why he repeatedly sought to have her feeding tube removed to allow her to die. Her parents, Mary and Robert Schindler, however, wanted to keep Terri alive at all costs, and they repeatedly fought Michael in the courts. Finally, on March 18, 2005, Terri's feeding tube was removed for the third and last time.

Prominent supporters of the decision to remove the feeding tube, many of whom were from the secular left, saw the Schiavo case in terms of rights, primarily the right to decide the manner of one's death. According to American Humanist Association executive director Tony Hileman, "Part of respecting the worth and dignity of life is respecting individual choice. A responsible society must honor Terri Schiavo's wishes." Political analyst Bill Press explained the importance of the right to die: "Terri Schiavo can't talk. She can't even think. She is only alive because she was hooked up to a feeding machine. By unplugging that machine, doctors are not killing her. They are letting her exercise the last right any of us have on earth: the right to die by natural causes."

Outspoken opponents of the decision to remove the feeding tube, many of whom were from the religious right, argued that since Terri Schiavo was not terminally ill, removing the feeding tube was tantamount to the murder of a disabled woman. They further described right-to-die advocates as proponents of a "culture of death." Randall Terry, founder of the antiabortion group Operation Rescue, became a spokesman for the Schindlers, who are conservative Catholics. He explicitly linked the Schiavo case with the antiabortion movement: "Obviously, the pro-life movement is saying it is unjust to kill an innocent child simply because that child lives in the womb. And we're saying, 'Whoa, wait a minute, it is unjust to starve a person to death simply because they're severely disabled.'"

Because the Florida courts had repeatedly ruled in favor of Michael Schiavo, the Republican-controlled Congress approved a bill allowing the Schindlers to take their legal challenge to federal court. Republican president George W. Bush flew from his Texas ranch to Washington to sign the bill into law. In remarks after signing the bill, the president explained his support: "The case of Terri Schiavo raises complex issues. Yet in instances like this one, where there are serious questions and substantial doubts, our society, our laws, and our courts should have a presumption in favor of life. Those who live at the mercy of others deserve our special care and concern. It should be our goal as a nation to build a culture of life, where all Americans are valued, welcomed, and protected—and that culture of life must extend to individuals with disabilities."

Political analyst Jack Cafferty, however, disagreed. "It's all about politics. It has nothing to do with Terri Schiavo. This is all about the abortion debate and right to life and the right wing of the Republican party." Congressman Ron Paul claimed that the Schiavo case should have remained a private matter. "In a free society the doctor and the patient—or his or her designated spokesperson—make the decision, short of using violence, in dealing with death and dying issues. The government stays out of it."

Polls after the bill was signed indicated surprisingly broad opposition to the government's action, even among self-described evangelical Christians, demonstrating that there is not unanimity on the "life issues"—abortion, euthanasia, and embryonic stem-cell research—even among conservative Christians. For example, some vociferous abortion foes, such as Senator Orrin Hatch of Utah, favor expanded federal funding for embryonic stem-cell research. His stance surprises many, for those opposed to abortion generally oppose embryonic stem-cell research, which results in the destruction of embryos. Some liberals, especially advocates for the rights of the disabled, sided with the right-to-life conservatives on the Schiavo case. Clearly, forming a consistent philosophy with regards to these controversial issues is challenging for people all along the political spectrum.

On March 31, 2005, Terri Schiavo died at the age of 41. Michael Schiavo's lawyer, right-to-die advocate George Felos, described her death as "calm, peaceful, and gentle." Ken Connor, however, an adviser to the Schindlers, said that society had abandoned Terri Schiavo. "The character of any culture is judged by the way we treat the weakest and most vulnerable among us," he said, arguing that Schiavo's death was a blot on America's character.

People on both sides of the controversy did agree that one positive resulted from the Schiavo case: a heightened interest in documenting end-of-life wishes in living wills and other legal instruments. Managers of Web sites offering such documents and instructions for filling them out reported massive increases in the number of people visiting their sites. Analysts point out that as more Americans document their end-of-life wishes, fewer cases like Schiavo's will occur.

All human beings must necessarily confront death, and the Schiavo case brought this reality home for many people. The authors in *At Issue: The Right to Die* explore the difficult choices that sometimes must be made at the end of life. Central to such discussions is whether individuals have the right to die as they wish or whether society has a vested interest in opposing all methods for hastening death.

1

People Have the Right to Control the Time and Manner of Their Death

Tom Flynn

Tom Flynn is the editor of Free Inquiry *and former coordinator of the First Amendment Task Force.*

In earlier times an individual's life belonged to the church or the state. Consequently, decisions relating to important events such as marriage, birth, and death were dictated by religious, governmental, or parental authorities. In modern times, however, people have autonomy and freedom of choice in important personal matters, including the right to choose their time of death.

Not long ago, the right to suicide and the right to assisted suicide seemed a single issue. Do individuals' lives belong to God, society, or themselves? For most humanists the answer was obvious. People own their lives; self-determination is a primary value. Therefore, society should get out of the way of rational suicides, letting them pursue their urgently held desires even unto death. We might not approve of their reasons, but what of that? It is they, not we, who choose to expend their highest asset. As [Romanian philosopher] E.M. Cioran observed, "Taking one's life is sufficiently impressive to forestall any petty hunt for motives."

This reflects a centuries-old emancipatory current in Western thought, roughly coeval with Renaissance humanism, which freed individuals from various social and ecclesiastical controls. Generations ago, your parents told you how you'd earn your living and whom you'd marry (until death, however miserably). Priests told you what to worship. Kings told you what to think. Your life belonged to God or the state; woe to any who dared resolve that they had lived enough. Suicide was a crime akin to poaching. There being no way to punish successful perpetrators, society could only lard on opprobrium, heightening the prospective cost to a suicide's survivors.

Freedom of Choice

Fast forward: today people choose their careers, their mates, change their religious views and their politics, and can think for themselves (a right too seldom exercised, but I digress). One archaic yoke remains: the conviction that whoever owns your life, it's not you. Hence suicide remains under that umbra of social denunciation from which divorce—or, say, marrying outside your social class—has but recently emerged. The prohibition of suicide may be the last of the ancien regime's curbs on self-determination.

That's why some humanist reformers defended suicide and euthanasia in the same breath. If your life is yours, then it is no one else's business if you choose to discontinue having experiences. If others yearn to offer relief to sufferers unable to end their own lives, there's no moral reason why they shouldn't.

The debate over physician-assisted suicide has since moved to safer territory. Centering on issues such as how much informed consent is enough or the role of pain management, it avoids the prickly question of suicide's licitness. With few advocates to protect it, the right of humans to dispose of the lives they own—the right to suicide as such—faces heavy attack.

The New Prohibitionists

Today's "New Prohibitionists" cloak themselves in science, arguing that all suicides result from potentially preventable chemical imbalances in the brain. In other words, the suicidal deserve no rights because they're crazy by definition. When science runs out, critics focus on the agony of those the suicide leaves behind.

Scientific American is not above publishing the odd article with a social or political agenda, but until a February 2003 article on suicide, I don't recall it throwing an in-house project to a staff editor with a personal axe to grind. Carol Ezzell begins her article

"Why? The Neuroscience of Suicide" as follows:

> In 1994, two days after returning from a happy family vacation, my 57-year-old mother put the muzzle of a handgun to her left breast and fired, drilling a neat and lethal hole through her heart— and, metaphorically, through our family's as well.

Well, you know where she stands. After more autobiography, Ezzell ably summarizes current findings about the brain structures and neurochemistry of suicides. But her subtext is clear: Because suicide is always the choice of a diseased mind, society must do everything possible to prevent it. Some bright day neuroscience may do away with suicide, after which unhinged self-murderers will never again drill metaphorical holes through their family's hearts.

The Demonization of Suicide

Ezzell never considers that the special anguish suicide carries for survivors is fueled primarily by the way our culture demonizes it. Less judgmental attitudes might empower loved ones to make peace more readily with a suicide's decision. Nor does she consider that suicide is sometimes a rational choice.

People own their lives; self-determination is a primary value.

I have something in common with Carol Ezzell. My mother suicided, too, exhausted by years of ill health that required only intermittent hospitalization but promised worse to come. She didn't qualify for physician-assisted suicide, but in retrospect her decision to end her life when she did was eminently rational. I regret only that she had to be so damned furtive about it, killing herself in a needlessly brutal way and without giving most who loved her an opportunity to share good-byes. Why?

Because society not only reviles suicide, it rescinds the autonomy and freedom of most persons known to be considering it.

People Own Their Lives

Ezzell portrays all suicides in a scientistic, pathologizing way that would only make that situation worse. The same tone pervades much rhetoric against physician-assisted suicide. No doubt some individuals do kill themselves because of clinical depression or other potentially treatable conditions. No doubt some who opt for physician-assisted suicide might choose otherwise with better pain control. But there's no grounds for supposing that all suicides spring from pathological causes. If suicide can ever be a rational choice, then the argument from self-determination still carries weight. And the wholesale preemptive curtailment of personal liberties in the name of suicide prevention should be unacceptable.

What's really in play here is the old dogma that individuals don't own their own lives. Physician-assisted suicide is but part of the issue. If we trust our fellow humans to choose their occupations, their significant others, their political persuasions, and their stances on religion, we should also defend their right to dispose of their most valuable possessions—their lives—even if disposing of life is precisely the choice they make.

2

Only God Should Decide the Time and Manner of a Person's Death

David A. Miller

David A. Miller is the senior pastor of Faith Presbyterian Church in Seminole, Florida, a congregation of more than eight hundred members. He earned his doctor of ministry degree from Fuller Theological Seminary.

Some doctors and ethicists argue that people have a right to die in order to prevent unnecessary suffering or when their quality of life has deteriorated to an unacceptable level. However, the arguments of right-to-die advocates are flawed. First, most pain can be alleviated with medication. Second, patients questioning their quality of life are often battling depression, which in many cases can be eased by counseling. Finally, those who attempt to determine when life is no longer worth living place quality of life above the sanctity of life. There can be no right to die because only God can determine when it is time for each person to die.

Editor's Note: The following viewpoint was originally delivered as a sermon at Faith Presbyterian Church on August 26, 2001.

"Let's get it over with." Those were the words that Debbie spoke to the doctor who stood by her bedside. You see,

Debbie had been vomiting relentlessly in reaction to a recent medication. She had wasted away to eighty pounds and was struggling and gasping for oxygen. Debbie had no hope of recovery.

The doctor reviewed Debbie's charts and evaluated her condition. He then had the nurse draw up twenty milligrams of morphine sulfate into a syringe. He smiled at Debbie and informed her that the nurse would give her something that would help her rest. Within five minutes, Debbie's respiration slowed, she lost consciousness and died.

The right to die is really the same thing as the right to suicide.

The story of Debbie appeared in the *New England Journal of Medicine* several years ago. It sparked a fierce debate about Debbie's right to die. Eventually this doctor would go on trial for murder. A Maryland physician by the name of Nelson Goodman made this comment in a newspaper editorial:

> It seems possible to me that the necessary players were all present to act out the final stage of a life certain to end very soon. There was a patient in possession of her mental faculties, enduring long and intolerable suffering; a loved one standing at the bedside all night holding her hand and a concerned physician, also at bedside, with adequate information to assess the situation and make a decision.

What would you have done if you were the doctor? What would you have done if someone you loved very much was the one in bed? What would be your response if you were the person in the throes of suffering and pain?

A Time to Die

The Book of Ecclesiastes tells us, to every thing there is a season and a time for every purpose under heaven. A time to be born and a time to die (Ecclesiastes 3:1,2). Unfortunately, this time to die does not always come gently. We may wish that it will come after a long life. When it finally arrives it will be fully anticipated. The process of dying will be brief and relatively pain-less. But, unfortunately, this is the exception and not the rule.

I'd like to have an important conversation with you this morning. Unfortunately, I've already had this conversation with some of you as you were watching your loved ones suffer or lie in coma. At such a time, you so want to relieve the suf-fering, but on the other hand, you are equally troubled by the thought that you pulled the plug that ended the life of your loved one. In the midst of this kind of confusion and pain, it's hard to think clearly and make your very best decision.

That's why I want to talk with you today so that when those times come—and the time to die will come for everyone here in this room this morning—you won't just simply make an emotional decision but one based on knowledge, faith and clear conviction.

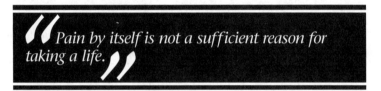

Pain by itself is not a sufficient reason for taking a life.

We truly never know when we're going to face this deci-sion. A young couple may think that they have nothing but happy days ahead until a child is born without a fully function-ing brain. We may have teenagers who seem to have the world by the tail. They're fulfilling all their promise and then a car ac-cident reduces them to a coma. There is the elderly person who is suffering through the final pangs of death. If death is in-evitable, why shouldn't they have the right to die?

Good Death

The Greeks had a word to describe this situation. They called it "euthanasia." This is a combination of the Greek words "eu" meaning good and "thanatos" meaning death. Is there such a thing as a good death? Do we have a right to die? What are the implications of this decision for those we love?

Before we try to answer this question, let's begin by making some very important distinctions that will sharpen the issues related to this difficult decision.

It's vitally important to understand the difference between passive and active euthanasia. Passive euthanasia involves a rejection of extraordinary and heroic and extreme medical means to keep someone alive who is facing imminent death. Passive euthanasia is allowing nature to take its course.

A key way to understand passive euthanasia is to ask the question, "What would have happened to the dying person a hundred years ago?" In that day people recognized that the time to die had come when the heart and the lungs and the brain began to shut down. They provided all of the care and comfort they could give and then let nature take its course.

But active euthanasia is something very different. Active euthanasia involves hastening death by using medical means to end life rather than to preserve it. Sometimes it may be administered through a lethal injection as was the situation with Debbie. Other times it may be withholding ordinary means such as feeding someone.

Another dimension of this is whether the choice to end life is voluntary or involuntary. . . . This analysis gives us four possible scenarios. Let's look at some examples to better understand these concepts.

Voluntary passive euthanasia can take place when the individual decides not to undergo another cancer treatment that would only delay an inevitable death.

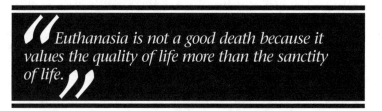

Euthanasia is not a good death because it values the quality of life more than the sanctity of life.

Involuntary passive euthanasia occurs when a loved one has had a stroke or perhaps a brain aneurysm. They've been rushed to the hospital and kept alive by a respirator as the diagnosis was being confirmed. The doctor informs you that if the respirator is removed, your loved one will die. There is no hope of recovery.

With this example it's important to note that the respirator is not so much sustaining life as it is prolonging death. Therefore the decision to remove the respirator is not an act of killing someone but rather letting someone die.

Active euthanasia, whether voluntary or involuntary, plays out in a very different way. Voluntary active euthanasia may occur where a person is living with a terminal illness but death is not imminent. There may be no cure for the disease but there are treatments available that can extend that person's life.

Assisted Suicide

Nonetheless the prospects of living life without a long-term future and only more painful medical treatments in the foreseeable near future, is a very discouraging prospect. Some become so discouraged they want to take their own life. If they ask a doctor to assist them in this process it is called assisted suicide.

Dr. Jack Kevorkian, nationally known for his crusade to legalize assisted suicide, believes that people have a right to die. This language may sound noble. But remember, the right to die is really the same thing as the right to suicide.

Permitting any form of active euthanasia poses great dangers. But the most dangerous form of euthanasia is that of involuntary active euthanasia. A disturbing example of this occurs when doctors and parents decide to stop feeding a one-day-old infant merely because the infant is born with Down syndrome.

But how do we know what future a life holds? Joni Eareckson Tada [a well-known advocate for the disabled] gave a wonderful testimony as to how our perspective can transform our limitations. But she did not always have this faith. When she realized she would be spending the rest of her life as a quadriplegic, she asked in despair, "Why can't they just let me die?" Her friend, Diane, tried to comfort her with the words, "The past is dead, Joni; you're alive." Joni responded, "Am I? This isn't living."

Aren't you glad that someone loved Joni through her depression and into the place of faith and hope in Christ?

This morning I would like to give you my personal reasons for opposing euthanasia. There may be many here who believe that you do have a right to die. While I will respect your right to disagree, let's together with an open mind take a look at what the Scriptures say on this vital matter.

Alleviating Pain

First of all, pain by itself is not a sufficient reason for taking a life. The Psalmist writes, Weeping may remain for a night but rejoicing comes in the morning (Psalm 30:5). As someone struggles through a disease or illness that has no cure, the level of pain will vary and change. What appears to be endless misery today may in fact be effectively managed tomorrow.

On one occasion I was teaching on this subject and a physician happened to be in attendance. I made the statement that there are drugs now available that can reduce to a satisfactory level any kind of suffering that we may face. Afterwards, the doctor came up to me and told me that based on his experience helping people in pain, he wholeheartedly agreed. The way he put it was, "Dave, I've got more medicine than you've got pain. I have always been able to help my patients—even those who are dying—to reduce their pain."

Further, it should be noted that often the person who is in pain is least likely to make a rational, well thought out decision. Pain is often associated with depression.

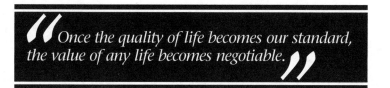

Once the quality of life becomes our standard, the value of any life becomes negotiable.

Going back to our opening illustration, I wonder if the doctor had the counseling skills to recognize whether Debbie had made a clearly thought through decision or whether she was going through a stage of depression that might later give way to hope.

Another critical factor is that "imminent death" is often difficult to determine despite the best of intentions. The doctors may be mistaken in their prognosis. The body may have some unexpected reserve capacity for healing and for regeneration. And then there's the possibility of new treatments and medicine that can suddenly brighten the prospects for the future.

Quality of Life vs. Value of Life

Secondly, euthanasia is not a good death because it values the quality of life more than the sanctity of life. Psalm 8 notes that because we have been created in God's image, we have been crowned with glory and honor (Psalm 8:5). God has crowned every human life with a glory and dignity, regardless of their status, achievement, net worth or beauty. This dignity becomes the common thread that binds us together and provides protection for the weak and the vulnerable.

On the other hand, once the quality of life becomes our

standard, the value of any life becomes negotiable. In our day the sanctity of life is coming under assault at the entrance gates and the exit gates of life. We question whether the life of an elderly person who's suffering dementia and barely functioning in a nursing home is the life that no longer has value. Others boldly ask whether the life of a handicapped newborn is a life worth living.

> *We begin to find ourselves putting a price tag on the value of a human soul.*

Those who want society to travel this path must face this question: "Who is going to define what qualities are necessary for a life to be protected?"

Peter Singer, a professor of ethics at Princeton University, is someone who is taken very seriously by respected medical journals and the academic community. Listen to how he defines quality of life:

> We can no longer base our ethics on the idea that human beings are a special form of creation, made in the image of God, singled out from all other animals and alone possessing an immortal soul. We should recognize that in some cases the life of a dog or a pig could be more morally significant than that of a defective infant, because the dog or pig might possess superior powers of rationality and self-consciousness. Mere membership in the species homo sapiens is not necessarily morally significant.

Cost-Benefit Approach to Life

But this is a very steep and slippery slope. Arguments for the quality of life can so easily give way to a "cost-benefit" approach to a human being. There are many people who feel that we are already spending too much money on people who are doing nothing more than just dying. Over twenty-five percent of all Medicare payments go to the elderly in the last years of their life. Eleven percent is spent on the last forty days! Those who are seeking to cut costs can see this as the ultimate in cost containment.

Now you may think that the only people who hold this kind of view are radical extremists. But consider these words spoken by Richard Lamb, the former governor of Colorado. He publicly stated that elderly people with terminal illness have a "duty to die and get out of the way." In more subtle ways, we find ourselves thinking, "If grandpa would just die, all of that money being spent on his illness could go for the kids' college education." Suddenly, we begin to find ourselves putting a price tag on the value of a human soul.

Involuntary Euthanasia

For the last decade the Netherlands has provided a test case for legalized euthanasia. Well-publicized studies have documented that over 1,000 people die every year from involuntary euthanasia. The physicians who presided over these deaths did not want to "disturb" the patients by asking their opinion on the matter. What guided their decision to end these lives? Thirty-one percent of the time it was because the person had a low quality of life. Thirty-two percent of the time, it was because the family could no longer take it. In other words, two-thirds of the time the intent of the patient had nothing to do with whether they continued living.

> *Euthanasia is wrong because we are called to leave the time of death in God's hands.*

Some people struggle to believe that their life is worth living because there is no one that really cares. There have been times in my ministry when someone has said to me, "Dave, I want to die and if I could take my life, I would." At such times, I have had the privilege of taking their hand and looking them in the eye and saying:

> The fact that you are facing your difficult circumstances and faith is an inspiration to me. And no matter how lost you think your life is, it means something to me and my life is enriched by knowing you.

This simple affirmation can be enough to give a person

[what they need] to want to go on living. I would encourage you to give this same affirmation. Rather than being the person who joins the chorus of voices that say your life doesn't count, why not be the person that gives them the affirmation they need to live out all the days that God has given them here on this earth?

In God's Hands

Thirdly, euthanasia is wrong because we are called to leave the time of death in God's hands. In 2 Corinthians, chapter 5, Paul shows us what it means to let Christ be Lord of the dying process. In verse two he honestly acknowledges that there are times when we groan, longing to be clothed with our heavenly dwelling (2 Corinthians 5:2). Going through the trials and suffering of life, we groan. When we become weighed down by the aches and pains of life, we groan.

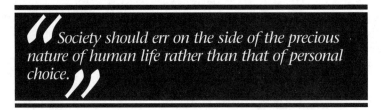

Society should err on the side of the precious nature of human life rather than that of personal choice.

But we groan knowing that there is a future hope. We are not frantically holding onto every ounce of life that we have in this world. Like Paul, we know that when God releases us from the grip of pain, we will be ushered into the presence of Christ. We know that to be absent from the body is to be present with the Lord (2 Corinthians 5:8).

Our future is so glorious we may be tempted to want to prematurely escape the pain and suffering associated with a terminal illness. But the Apostle Paul comes to just the opposite conclusion. He goes on to affirm that as long as God gives us breath we live by faith, not by sight (2 Corinthians 5:7). Sight would tell us that there is no hope. Just by continuing to live we place a financial burden on others. Living by sight we recognize that as we grow older, the dying process destroys our mind and robs us of our dignity. We are engulfed in pain and in every way it may seem that God has forgotten us.

But living by faith is completely different. By faith we affirm with the psalmist, my times are in your hands (Psalm 31:15). By faith we believe that the hand of God is guiding our life all the way to our final breath. By faith we believe that God will sustain us and those that we love in that difficult hour. By faith we understand that part of living is dying. By faith we affirm that no matter what season of life, whether we are at home in the body or away, we make it our goal to please him (2 Corinthians 5:9).

A Second Chance

I began with a story with a doctor who made a decision to take life. Dr. Alva B. Wier, an oncologist in Germantown, Tennessee, tells a similar story with a very different outcome. She writes of how she was awakened one night by a distraught mother who told her that her son, a cancer patient, had just tried to commit suicide by swallowing a bottle of sleeping pills. Sadly this young man was in the final stages of cancer. A few minutes later she met the mother in the Emergency Room. At first the mother asked the doctor to just let her son die in peace. But the doctor urged her to at least give him a chance at life. With mixed emotions the mother agreed.

Here's how Dr. Wier described what happened after that:

> I admitted him, expecting him to die. The following weekend I was surprised to find this man's name on my list. I walked into the room to find a beaming mother and an alert patient. With the minimal support, he had survived his overdose. After another week, he was walking with his pain improved . . . and depression diminished.
>
> I realized that this man and his family were experiencing moments together of unfathomable value.

There is no one this side of heaven who has the ability to make the correct decision regarding when our life should be extinguished. Society should err on the side of the precious nature of human life rather than that of personal choice.

3

Euthanasia and Physician-Assisted Suicide Should Be Legal

Lawrence Rudden

Lawrence Rudden is director of research for the Graham Williams Group, a public relations firm in Washington, D.C. He writes on politics and culture.

The state of Oregon enacted the Death with Dignity Act in 1997, which made it the first state to legalize physician-assisted suicide. However, the U.S. Department of Justice has challenged the law on the grounds that prescribing drugs to be used in an assisted suicide is not a legitimate medical purpose for those drugs. Critics of the Oregon law point to the Netherlands, where legalized physician-assisted suicide has led to euthanizing disabled or mentally ill patients who are not terminally ill. These analysts worry that the same practices will eventually occur in the United States if laws such as Oregon's are enacted. However, the Oregon law is carefully crafted to prevent abuse. The government should not interfere in the most intimate and personal decision of citizens—the choice to end their lives.

Evelyn was diagnosed with breast cancer in 1997. She spent the next four years dying.

At first she waged war on the cancer, attacking her own body with radiation and pills until she was left inhabiting something limp and unresponsive. Still, the cancer continued to grow inside her, replicating through her spine, shoulders, hips, pelvis, and liver.

She watched as her body began to fail her. There were awful waves of pain, violent coughing, constipation, abdominal cramps, convulsions, and humiliation. She had trouble breathing and walking. The sickness was overwhelming her.

> *In 1997, Oregon passed the Death with Dignity Act, making it the only state to permit physician-assisted suicide.*

Evelyn was moved to an assisted living facility, where she was told she had less than six months to live. Plastic tubes were strung up, around and through her body. She lay on her hospital bed like a wax figure. There was nothing heroic about barely persisting.

Evelyn had seen her mother die a horrible, cringing death. She did not want that for herself. She wanted to die with dignity. On September 24, 2001, Evelyn asked the hospice nurse to help end her life. The nurse provided her with a number for Compassion in Dying, a nonprofit organization that supports the right of terminally ill patients to hasten their deaths. It agreed to help. Evelyn thought about having her family and medical personnel with her as she ended her life. This made her happy. On November 27, 2001, she swallowed a glass of liquid medication, slipped immediately into a coma, and died fifteen minutes later, at the age of seventy-two. Two days earlier, she had written a letter: "On Thanksgiving, I hope everyone in my family will take time to feel thankful that I live in Oregon and have the means to escape this cancer before it gets any worse. I love you all."

Oregon Law

In 1997, Oregon passed the Death with Dignity Act, making it the only state to permit physician-assisted suicide. Since then, the act has survived an attempt by Congress to overturn it, court hearings on its constitutional validity, and two voter initiatives, in which Oregon residents approved the measure first by a slim margin in 1994, then overwhelmingly in 1997. To qualify for assistance, patients must make two oral requests and one written request at least two weeks apart, be terminally ill with less than six months to live, and be judged mentally competent to make the decision by two separate physicians. Patients are also required to administer the medication themselves. Court records indicate that ninety-one people—mostly cancer patients—have used the provision to end their lives.

"Oregon's law is written with safeguards that prevent patients from using the law prematurely or impulsively," says George Eighmey, executive director of the Oregon branch of the Compassion in Dying Federation. According to Eighmey, patients have sought to end their lives primarily to avoid the profound loss of bodily control and dignity that often accompanies the late stages of a terminal illness.

Can the federal government deny this opportunity to spend one's final months or days in a manner that one does not consider repulsive? According to Attorney General John Ashcroft, it not only can but should. The nation's highest lawyer has declared that assisted suicide is not a "legitimate medical purpose"; in between leading the war on terror, he has been hard at work attempting to punish Oregon doctors for prescribing medications intended to help terminally ill patients end their lives.

> *Can the federal government deny this opportunity to spend one's final months or days in a manner that one does not consider repulsive?*

In November 2001, Ashcroft declared that any doctor who prescribed lethal doses of painkilling medication with the specific intent of ending his patient's life would lose his license to prescribe medications and would serve a mandatory twenty-year sentence. He defended this ultimatum on the vague grounds that doctors prescribing lethal doses of painkilling medication were in violation of the federal Controlled Substances Act (CSA), a statute intended to punish illicit trafficking of pharmaceuticals.

Supporters of the Ashcroft directive are fond of observing that it does not actually forbid doctors from helping patients end their lives. "Oregon's physicians could still practice assisted suicide, but they could not prescribe federally controlled substances for that purpose," explains Rita Marker, executive director of the International Task Force on Euthanasia and Assisted Suicide. In other words, doctors would still be free to prescribe, say, lethal doses of rat poison to Oregon's dying citizens. For obvious reasons—medical ethics, fear of lawsuits, the semblance of something resembling empathy and compassion—this will not happen. Nor, for that matter, would a doctor who had his license to prescribe drugs stripped under the Ashcroft directive be likely to remain a doctor for long. "For an oncologist to be unable to prescribe pain medication is incomprehensible," explains Oregon's Dr. Peter Rasmussen. "I would have to retire. . . . I want to continue to be a practicing physician. I would not be able to help my patients." So, despite some semantic zigzagging, the effect of the directive is really quite straightforward: to prevent states from experimenting with the practice of physician-assisted suicide.

> *Denied the opportunity for physician-assisted suicide, some patients chose a more violent way of ending their lives.*

Psychiatrist Greg Hamilton, of Portland's Physicians for Compassionate Care group, thinks this is plainly a good thing. "Helping a patient to die is to spend time with the patient and to treat his symptoms. It's not to overdose the patient. That's not helping a patient during his dying process. That's murdering the patient."

Desperate for Relief

Many of Oregon's dying and their family members are less enthusiastic about forcing terminal patients to die slowly, in pain and without dignity. Linda Kilcrease watched as cancerous tumors wrapped around the blood vessels in her mother's neck, slowly constricting the flow of blood to and from the brain. "Her death was a race between her brain slowly exploding in one stroke after another when blood could not drain from her head, or her heart exploding trying to pump more blood into her head. . . . We watched as her head blew up like a balloon, forcing her eyes closed. When the blood first began to back up and could not drain, we watched as her heart began to beat so hard and fast, nearly ripping through her chest, trying to get blood into her head. The hospital staff gave us heartbeat and blood pressure monitors and we watched the wild fluctuations in vital statistics. We learned how to position Mom's head so her heart would calm down. We watched her change from a robust woman to a shriveled skeleton. . . . It was torture for everyone, but especially Mom. . . . Those who say pain medication and psychiatric help are all that is needed to help someone facing death have it all wrong. Neither would be of any use to my mother."

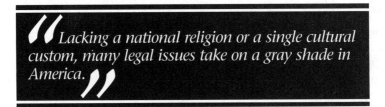

Lacking a national religion or a single cultural custom, many legal issues take on a gray shade in America.

Denied the opportunity for physician-assisted suicide, some patients chose a more violent way of ending their lives. During the late stages of Emanuel McGeorge's cancer, he often found himself in a stupor from the morphine that was being pumped into his veins. A fiercely independent man, McGeorge worried that he was losing control over his life. "Mac did not want to be a sedated vegetable," recalls his wife, Patsy. And so one day he handed her a note, kissed her weathered cheek, then stumbled into the front yard, where he carefully lodged a shotgun in his mouth and pulled the trigger.

By providing terminal patients with the opportunity to die peacefully, under medical care and with loved ones present, the Death with Dignity Act "has prevented more than fifty-seven people from committing violent suicides during the past five years," says Eighmey.

Government Interference

Theoretically, the matter of physician-assisted suicide should be left to the states, as indicated by a 1997 Supreme Court ruling. "Throughout the nation," observed Chief Justice William Rehnquist in his majority opinion, "Americans are engaged in an earnest and profound debate about the morality, legality, and practicality of physician-assisted suicide. Our holding permits this debate to continue, as it should in a democratic society."

Having seemingly arrived at the principle that physician-assisted suicide is wrong, Ashcroft will be damned if he's going to allow the terminal patients of Oregon to exercise their legal right to end their unbearable suffering. Without so much as providing notice to Oregon officials or the general public, he has declared the practice "not medically legitimate," raising concerns that the country's top lawyer is being guided not by the nuances of law but rather by the moral certainties of personal ideology.

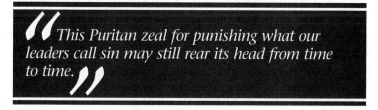

This Puritan zeal for punishing what our leaders call sin may still rear its head from time to time.

Of course, personal ideology is an admittedly imprecise thing, and attempts by the government to dictate what is good for the character of the nation raise a more difficult question: to whose ideology should the law adhere? Lacking a national religion or a single cultural custom, many legal issues take on a gray shade in America. Plainly, this is a good thing. History indicates that when the law and personal ideology get too close, the law often becomes a straightjacket to individual liberties. The Nazis maintained their power in part by using vague moral codes to destroy any threat to their power base. More recently, the Taliban [ruling regime in Afghanistan] used the law to punish all variety of sinners, from the heretics to the merely thoughtful. Early on, America's Puritan founders were also hard at work persecuting their neighbors for real and imagined shortcomings—a fact that continues to find expression in the numerous state codes regulating sexual conduct.

Though in general practice our society now tends to keep a proper distance between the law and personal ideology, this Puritan zeal for punishing what our leaders call sin may still rear its head from time to time. Exhibit A: Ashcroft's attempt to invalidate Oregon's Death with Dignity Act. Ashcroft carried the same tune while in Congress, where he twice supported legislation that would subject doctors to twenty years in prison if they prescribed federally regulated drugs to cause a patient's death. Both times the legislation failed.

Now, as attorney general, he is again insisting that physician-assisted suicide is "not a legitimate medical practice," an assessment he defends by observing that doctors are charged with helping patients live, not making them dead. Very good. Nevertheless, the Court has already allowed the administration of "risky pain relief," that is, doses of pain relief that are likely to hasten the death of a terminally ill patient. Is this procedure somehow more "legitimate" than assisted suicide? Is it medically legitimate to deny someone a right to die with dignity? Is such a right "fundamental" to patients whose condition is so severe that pain-relief medication is not sufficient to relieve their suffering? Is it somehow more medically legitimate to have politicians second-guessing doctors? And might strict federal oversight of doctors who prescribe pain medication actually have the broader effect of scaring them into undermedicating dying patients? These are all terribly complicated questions, though Ashcroft doesn't seem to mind ducking his head and smashing right through them.

States' Rights

Along the way, Ashcroft has set the stage for a classic battle of states' versus federal rights. Since Oregon doctors are prescribing federally controlled medications to help Oregon residents kill themselves, the Justice Department claims jurisdiction over the process. It argues that the CSA authorizes the attorney general to revoke a practitioner's license to prescribe medications, if he determines that the practitioner is acting in a manner that "threatens public health," regardless of state laws.

> *An individual should not be forced to spend his final days in excruciating pain simply because this is what his neighbor feels is right.*

Advocates of states' rights maintain that Ashcroft is expanding the scope of the CSA beyond its original intent—regulating the illegal sale of pharmaceuticals. They also dispute that he has the authority to determine whether physician-assisted suicide constitutes "a legitimate medical practice" and quiver at the idea of an unelected, unaccountable government official dictating some of the most personal decisions of their lives. This intrusion, they maintain, is a violation of the spirit of the Constitution.

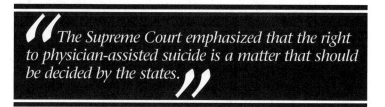

The Supreme Court emphasized that the right to physician-assisted suicide is a matter that should be decided by the states.

Round 1 went to the states' advocates. In his harshly critical rebuke of the Ashcroft directive, Oregon federal judge Robert Jones wrote that it would be "unprecedented and extraordinary" for Congress to assign the attorney general the authority to interpret what constitutes a legitimate medical practice. While Jones acknowledged that Ashcroft may be "fully justified, morally, ethically, religiously," in opposing assisted suicide, he emphasized that the attorney general's strong feelings alone do "not permit a federal statute to be manipulated from its true meaning, even to satisfy a worthy goal."

Intrepidly, the Justice Department carries on. On September 25, 2001, it filed an appeal with the Ninth U.S. Circuit Court of Appeals—the same court that previously ruled that the due process clause of the Fourteenth Amendment prevents the government from flatly banning physician-assisted suicide. The case will be heard in spring 2003, after which an appeal to the U.S. Supreme Court is expected. [The Supreme Court is expected to rule in October 2005].

Supreme Court Precedence and Individual Rights

In their 1997 ruling, the Supreme Court justices voted 9–0 that terminal patients do not have a generalized constitutional right to physician-assisted suicide. The ruling applied only to the cases before the Court and did not take into account the Oregon law. At the same time, the justices littered their opinions with enough qualifiers about specific constitutional rights and principles to effectively make a tangled mess of things. Justice [David] Souter, for example, noted that a total ban on physician-assisted suicide could in fact be deemed unconstitutional if it violated certain basic and historically protected principles of personal autonomy. He added that there exist arguments of "increasing forcefulness for recognizing some right to a doctor's help in suicide." Justice [Stephen] Breyer emphasized that forcing dying patients to live out their final days in great pain might violate a general right "to die with dignity." Justice [John Paul] Stevens wrote a separate opinion in which he plainly stated that if presented with an appropriate case, he would overrule a ban on physician-assisted suicide. In effect, Stevens recalled that our country does not have a national religion or culture. As our multicultural melange of citizens may have very different moral, religious, or personal ideas about how they ought to spend their final days, terminal patients should have the freedom to pursue these convictions so long as their actions affect only their own morality. In other words, an individual should not be forced to spend his final days in excruciating pain simply because this is what his neighbor feels is right.

During a recent speech on Oregon's physician-assisted suicide law, Justice [Antonin] Scalia was even more straightforward: "You want the right to die," snorted Justice Scalia to his audience at the Northwestern School of Law of Lewis and Clark College. "That's right and that's fine. You don't hear me complaining about Oregon's law."

So, what to do? The Supreme Court emphasized that the right to physician-assisted suicide is a matter that should be decided by the states. Indeed, the democratization of this issue would have the beneficial effect of making real-world experience relevant to the law. Rather than freezing the law in accordance with the speculation of political or religious groups, we could learn from experience in a systematic fashion and thus make law adaptive to the individual needs of terminal patients.

The Example of the Netherlands

For critics, experimentation with physician-assisted suicide would come at the unacceptable cost of making terminally ill patients vulnerable to increased pressure to end their lives—either by profit-oriented HMOs [health maintenance organizations] or out of implicit guilt for the financial and emotional burden they are exacting on relatives. "In an era of cost control and managed care, patients with lingering illnesses may be branded an economic liability, and decisions to encourage death can be driven by cost," says Cathy Cleaver of the U.S. Conference of Catholic Bishops. Cleaver points to the Netherlands, where physician-assisted suicide is legal and occurring at an alarming rate: "For years Dutch courts have allowed physicians to practice euthanasia and assisted suicide with impunity, supposedly only in cases where desperately ill patients have unbearable suffering. In a few years, however, Dutch policy and practice have expanded to allow the killing of people with disabilities or even physically healthy people with psychological distress; thousands of patients have been killed by their doctors without their request. The Dutch example teaches us that the 'slippery slope' is very real."

In short, Cleaver worries that if we let doctors end the pointless suffering of terminal patients, the practice would quickly become the norm. Soon depressed people would be demanding a right to die, our palliative-care options would begin to lag behind the rest of the civilized world, and our doctors would be transformed into stalking butchers. An alarming thought, but just one thing: For years the Dutch had almost no formalized procedure in place to regulate the process. Physicians were expected to report themselves to a governing board, which would determine after the fact whether they had broken the law.

By contrast, Oregon's law requires extensive reporting requirements, and, after five years, "evidence points to 100 percent reporting compliance and no deviation from the rules in Oregon," says Barbara Coombs Lee, president of the Compassion in Dying Federation. In fact, a survey of Oregon physicians who have had experience with the Death with Dignity Act reports that some candidates are being screened out of the program. According to the study, only 29 (18 percent) of the 165 people who had requested medication under the act actually received a prescription.

For those who did receive one, control over their final few days, not access to healing options, was the point. It is unlikely that critics will pause long enough to acknowledge this rousing fact. Even at this late date, some of our highest government officials remain dedicated to the idea of regulating the most intimate decisions of this country's citizens, even when the outcome affects only the morality of the actor.

Truly, that is alarming.

4

Euthanasia and Physician-Assisted Suicide Should Not Be Legal

Margaret Somerville

Margaret Somerville is a professor on the faculty of medicine of McGill University. She is also the Gale Professor of Law.

There are two reasons why euthanasia should not be legalized. One, allowing the practice would undermine society's respect for human life and death. Second, legalizing euthanasia would damage medicine by transforming doctors from healers into killers. Taking these two reasons into account, it is clear that permitting terminally ill people to choose euthanasia would eventually lead to the killing of society's most vulnerable citizens without their consent.

There are two major reasons to oppose euthanasia. One is based on principle: it is wrong for one human to intentionally kill another (except in justified self-defense, or in the defense of others). The other reason is utilitarian: the harms and risks of legalizing euthanasia, to individuals in general and to society, far outweigh any benefits.

When personal and societal values were largely consistent with each other, and widely shared because they were based on a shared religion, the case against euthanasia was simple: God

Margaret Somerville, "The Case Against Euthanasia and Physician-Assisted Suicide," *Free Inquiry*, vol. 23, Spring 2003, pp. 33–34. Copyright © 2003 by Council for Democratic and Secular Humanism, Inc. Reproduced by permission.

or the gods (and, therefore, the religion) commanded "Thou shalt not kill." In a secular society, especially one that gives priority to intense individualism, the case for euthanasia is simple: Individuals have the right to choose the manner, time, and place of their death. In contrast, in such societies the case against euthanasia is complex.

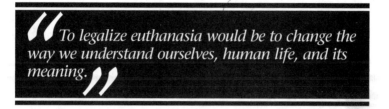

To legalize euthanasia would be to change the way we understand ourselves, human life, and its meaning.

Definitions are a source of confusion in the euthanasia debate—some of it deliberately engendered by euthanasia advocates to promote their case. Euthanasia is "a deliberate act that causes death undertaken by one person with the primary intention of ending the life of another person, in order to relieve that person's suffering." Euthanasia is not the justified withdrawing or withholding of treatment that results in death. And it is not the provision of pain relief, even if it could or would shorten life, provided the treatment is necessary to relieve the patient's pain or other serious symptoms of physical distress and is given with a primary intention of relieving pain and not of killing the patient.

Secular Arguments Against Euthanasia

1. Impact on society. To legalize euthanasia would damage important, foundational societal values and symbols that uphold respect for human life. With euthanasia, how we die cannot be just a private matter of self-determination and personal beliefs, because euthanasia "is an act that requires two people to make it possible and a complicit society to make it acceptable." The prohibition on intentional killing is the cornerstone of law and human relationships, emphasizing our basic equality.

Medicine and the law are the principal institutions that maintain respect for human life in a secular, pluralistic society. Legalizing euthanasia would involve—and harm—both of them. In particular, changing the norm that we must not kill each other would seriously damage both institutions' capacity to carry the value of respect for human life.

To legalize euthanasia would be to change the way we understand ourselves, human life, and its meaning. To explain this last point requires painting a much larger picture. We create our values and find meaning in life by buying into a "shared story"—a societal-cultural paradigm. Humans have always focused that story on the two great events of each life, birth and death. Even in a secular society—indeed, more than in a religious one—that story must encompass, create space for, and protect the "human spirit." By the human spirit, I do not mean anything religious (although this concept can accommodate the religious beliefs of those who have them). Rather, I mean the intangible, invisible, immeasurable reality that we need to find meaning in life and to make life worth living— that deeply intuitive sense of relatedness or connectedness to others, the world, and the universe in which we live.

There are two views of human life and, as a consequence, death. One is that we are simply "gene machines." In the words of an Australian politician, when we are past our "best before" or "use by" date, we should be checked out as quickly, cheaply and efficiently as possible. That view favors euthanasia. The other view sees a mystery in human death, because it sees a mystery in human life, a view that does not require any belief in the supernatural.

> *[Euthanasia] converts the mystery of death to the problem of death, to which we then seek a technological solution.*

Euthanasia is a "gene machine" response. It converts the mystery of death to the problem of death, to which we then seek a technological solution. A lethal injection is a very efficient, fast solution to the problem of death—but it is antithetical to the mystery of death. People in postmodern societies are uncomfortable with mysteries, especially mysteries that generate intense, free-floating anxiety and fear, as death does. We seek control over the event that elicits that fear; we look for a terror-management or terror-reduction mechanism. Euthanasia is such a mechanism: While it does not allow us to avoid the cause of our fear—death—it does allow us to control its manner, time, and place—we can feel that we have death under control.

Giving Hope

Research has shown that the marker for people wanting euthanasia is a state that psychiatrists call "hopelessness," which they differentiate from depression—these people have nothing to look forward to. Hope is our sense of connection to the future; hope is the oxygen of the human spirit. Hope can be elicited by a sense of connection to a very immediate future, for instance, looking forward to a visit from a loved person, seeing the sun come up, or hearing the dawn chorus. When we are dying, our horizon comes closer and closer, but it still exists until we finally cross over. People need hope if they are to experience dying as the final great act of life, as it should be. Euthanasia converts that act to an act of death.

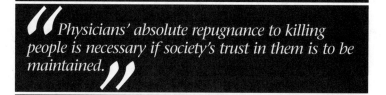

Physicians' absolute repugnance to killing people is necessary if society's trust in them is to be maintained.

A more pragmatic, but nevertheless very important, objection to legalizing euthanasia is that its abuse cannot be prevented, as recent reports on euthanasia in the Netherlands have documented. Indeed, as a result of this evidence some former advocates now believe that euthanasia cannot be safely legalized and have recently spoken against doing so.

To assess the impact that legalizing euthanasia might have, in practice, on society, we must look at it in the context in which it would operate: The combination of an aging population, scarce health-care resources, and euthanasia would be a lethal one.

Damage to Medicine

2. Impact on medicine. Advocates often argue that euthanasia should be legalized because physicians are secretly carrying it out anyway. Studies purporting to establish that fact have recently been severely criticized on the grounds that the respondents replied to questions that did not distinguish between actions primarily intended to shorten life—euthanasia—and other acts or omissions in which no such intention was present—pain-relief treatment or refusals of treatment—that are not euthanasia. But even if the studies were accurate, the fact that physicians are secretly carrying out euthanasia does not mean that it is right. Further, if physicians were presently ignoring the law against murder, why would they obey guidelines for voluntary euthanasia?

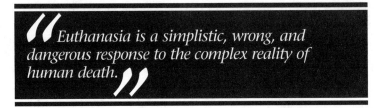

Euthanasia is a simplistic, wrong, and dangerous response to the complex reality of human death.

Euthanasia "places the very soul of medicine on trial." Physicians' absolute repugnance to killing people is necessary if society's trust in them is to be maintained. This is true, in part, because physicians have opportunities to kill not open to other people, as the horrific story of Dr. Harold Shipman, the British physician-serial killer, shows.

How would legalizing euthanasia affect medical education? What impact would physician role models carrying out euthanasia have on medical students and young physicians? Would we devote time to teaching students how to administer death through lethal injection? Would they be brutalized or ethically desensitized? (Do we adequately teach pain-relief treatment at present?) It would be very difficult to communicate to future physicians a repugnance to killing in a context of legalized euthanasia.

Physicians need a clear line that powerfully manifests to them, their patients, and society that they do not inflict death; both their patients and the public need to know with absolute certainty—and to be able to trust—that this is the case. Anything that would blur the line, damage that trust, or make physicians less sensitive to their primary obligations to protect life is unacceptable. Legalizing euthanasia would do all of these things.

Euthanasia Is Wrong

Euthanasia is a simplistic, wrong, and dangerous response to the complex reality of human death. Physician-assisted suicide and euthanasia involve taking people who are at their weakest and most vulnerable, who fear loss of control or isolation and abandonment—who are in a state of intense "pre-mortem

loneliness"—and placing them in a situation where they believe their only alternative is to be killed or kill themselves.

Nancy Crick, a sixty-nine-year-old Australian grandmother,
recently committed suicide in the presence of over twenty
people, eight of whom were members of the Australian Voluntary Euthanasia Society. She explained: "I don't want to die
alone." Another option for Mrs. Crick (if she had been terminally ill—an autopsy showed Mrs. Crick's colon cancer had not
recurred) should have been to die naturally with people who
cared for her present and good palliative care.

Of people who requested assisted suicide under Oregon's
Death with Dignity Act, which allows physicians to prescribe
lethal medication, 46 percent changed their minds after significant palliative-care interventions (relief of pain and other
symptoms), but only 15 percent of those who did not receive
such interventions did so.

How a society treats its weakest, most in need, most vulnerable members best tests its moral and ethical tone. To set a present and future moral tone that protects individuals in general
and society, upholds the fundamental value of respect for life,
and promotes rather than destroys our capacities and opportunities to search for meaning in life, we must reject euthanasia.

5

Euthanasia Is Compassionate

Beth Dalbey

Beth Dalbey is editorial director for Business Publications Corp.

Euthanizing sick and dying pets is considered compassionate. The same compassion should be shown to sick and dying human beings. However, while many people accept euthanasia for pets, they find euthanasia for people morally objectionable. All creatures should be allowed to die without undue suffering. Physician-assisted suicide should be legal.

Gracie was a good cat who asked for nothing save pure love and gave nothing but pure love in return during our six years together. She deserved no less.

She was rescued from a miserable, feral existence in a junked car and was sheltered by people who recognized the value in all forms of life. No one disputes that she chose me. With a pair of green eyes that looked like extra-fancy olives dwarfing her tiny face and a mouth that looked perpetually turned up in a smile, she gazed at me demurely and distracted me from other cats that, frankly, looked healthier and less fragile. I was ready to adopt a plump, handsome black-and-white cat, but this petite gray tabby seemed to need me more.

They called her Kiki at the shelter, but the moment our eyes connected, I knew her name was Grace, a quality she possessed in spades. The kind of cat even the most passionate cat-haters found sweetly irresistible, she met only one person she did not like. She didn't slink away in fear, but pulled her slight, 7-pound frame into a ferocious arch and hissed at the person, who, it turned out, was no friend at all.

Compassion for Animals

Like her name, she was grace itself. In the end, I did only what grace would allow me to do. I let her go gently and with dignity; sparing her the pain and suffering of complete kidney failure and slow starvation. The choice was at the same time difficult and easy. How could I subject Gracie, who had brought so much joy into my life, to an agonizing and painful death because I wasn't ready to say goodbye?

I held her still body and felt enveloped by peace and a sense that I helped the natural order triumph over the science that would have kept her alive, but could never have given her life quality. Euthanasia (originating from the Greek language, where "eu" means "good" and "thanatos" means "death") for my companion was the right choice.

Cruelty for People

That choice I and so many other animal lovers have made for mercy is universally viewed as laudable, selfless, compassionate, virtuous and loving. It occurred to me—and so many people have remarked in recent days—that our values have been turned upside down when this simple act of love we encourage for our terminally ill pets is denied for our human loved ones, whose impact in our lives is far more profound. To prolong the lives of dying pets is considered cruel and selfish; for a person to opt for a painless exit when death is inevitable and imminent, when suffering is unbearable and pain excruciating, and when no path of treatment remains open, is morally objectionable to many.

No one's talking about genocide, or imposing the choice on individuals who do not expressly request it. The crime isn't assisted suicide, but that it is considered a crime.

Everyone deserves to die with grace.

6

Euthanasia Is Not Compassionate

Wesley J. Smith

Wesley J. Smith is a senior fellow at the Discovery Institute and an attorney for the International Task Force on Euthanasia and Assisted Suicide.

Advocates of euthanasia claim that the practice is compassionate. However, as the case of the Netherlands, where euthanasia is legal, illustrates, when euthanasia for terminally ill people is accepted, soon the practice spreads to those who are not seriously ill. Dutch doctors now help Alzheimer's patients die, for example. Killing Alzheimer's sufferers, who can still love and be loved, is cruel. The compassionate approach to dealing with such sufferers would be to care for them until their natural deaths.

Compassion, literally defined, means, "to suffer with another." That is why I have always found the monopolization of that word by proponents of euthanasia and assisted suicide so discordant. Euthanasia isn't about suffering *with* anybody. It's about using someone's suffering—and the pity it evokes—as a justification to kill.

The Netherlands has allowed euthanasia for more than 30 years, supposedly under strict guidelines to protect the vulnerable from abuse. But the list of those "eligible" has steadily lengthened, to the point that it now includes depressed people without organic illnesses. And now, the Dutch government has opened the legal door to killing patients with Alzheimer's disease. In doing so, the nation sent a powerful message to Alzheimer's patients and their families: The lives of those with this dreaded disease are so burdensome and undignified that they are not worth maintaining or protecting.

True Compassion

Contrast this with the message Nancy Reagan [widow of the late president Ronald Reagan] and her family sent the world by lovingly caring for Ronald Reagan in his declining years. This is what true compassion looks like. Through their unwavering devotion—giving wholeheartedly to Reagan even when he had little to give back in return, and taking some of his suffering on their own shoulders for ten difficult years—the Reagan family provided a vivid demonstration of the power of unconditional love. Nothing that has been done to recognize the late president—the naming of an airport after him, the public outpouring of respect during the week of mourning, the burying of political hatchets—could have honored Ronald Reagan the man, husband, and father more appropriately.

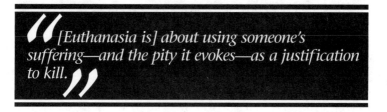

[Euthanasia is] about using someone's suffering—and the pity it evokes—as a justification to kill.

Ronald Reagan understood clearly how crucial it is to value all people equally, regardless of their capacities or state of health. Writing in *Human Life Review* in 1983, in words that are especially poignant considering what befell him ten years later, he warned:

> Regrettably, we live at a time when some persons do not value all human life. They want to pick and choose which individuals have value. Some have said that only those individuals with "consciousness of self" are human beings.

This dehumanization offended Reagan to his core. He warned that the philosophy established at the Founding of the United States that all are created equal, possessing an inalienable right to life, is subverted when some of us are seen as disposable. And he recognized that sanctioning their killing—even in a desire to alleviate suffering—undermines our essential humanity.

Profound Meaning in Life

Of course, some would say that the reverse is true, that a life with Alzheimer's isn't really living. Better to put people out of their misery than allow them to die slowly, while losing their identities. Such an end is seen as especially burdensome for those who have lived robust lives of independence, intellectual rigor, achievement, and accomplishment—people who would be humiliated to see themselves having to depend so totally on others for their care.

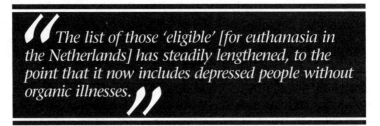

The list of those 'eligible' [for euthanasia in the Netherlands] has steadily lengthened, to the point that it now includes depressed people without organic illnesses.

But the life Reagan led in his declining years demonstrates how wrongheaded such views are. True, Reagan was no longer able to occupy the public stage. True, he was very ill. True, this caused him and his family tremendous anguish. But it is untrue that falling prey to catastrophic illness meant that he possessed less human dignity and moral worth than he did when telling [Soviet leader] Mikhail Gorbachev to "tear down this [Berlin] wall." Indeed, what we have learned . . . about Reagan's gentle life in his final, private years demonstrates that there can be profound meaning even in the most difficult and trying circumstances.

Betsy Streisand's "Memories of a Friend in the Park," a first-person observation piece published in the June 21, 2004 *U.S. News & World Report*, was especially touching in this regard. Streisand recounts how, as Reagan's Alzheimer's forced him out of the public limelight in the late 1990s, he frequented a park in Beverly Hills. Reagan, accompanied by his nurse, liked to sit on a park bench and watch children at play. She recalled:

> Reagan didn't speak much to adults. It was our children he was interested in. Time and again these

sticky little specimens encrusted with juice and sand would come up next to him as they made their way to the bags of snacks on the bench. And he would beckon them closer. . . . And although he gradually stopped speaking to us—and our children—we never stopped speaking to him or having the kids play close by where he could watch.

The Desire to Love

As Reagan's cognitive and verbal abilities collapsed, his human desire to love and be loved remained undiminished. Reagan's son Michael spoke emotionally to this when he described his dad's joy at hugging and being hugged. "As the years went by and he could no longer recognize me," Michael said in a tribute to his father, "I began a process of hugging him whenever I would see him." Most poignantly, the son recalled once forgetting to hug his father goodbye. As he was about to get into his car, Michael's wife told him to turn around. There in the doorway was Ronald Reagan, arms outstretched, waiting for his hug. Tears in his eyes, Michael rushed back to his father and the two embraced.

> *[Ronald Reagan] recognized that sanctioning . . . killing—even in a desire to alleviate suffering— undermines our essential humanity.*

Even at the very end, love triumphed over disease. Reagan loved his Nancy deeply and intensely, and as he was breathing his last breaths, somehow, some way, he dug deep within himself and found some final reserve of devotion. He opened his eyes, recognized her, and giving her one final look, he died. Nancy Reagan and the family called his final great communication a "wonderful gift."

The Brutality of Euthanasia

Now juxtapose this story of anguish—as well as love, grace, and devotion—with euthanasia in the Netherlands, which will now be applied to patients with Alzheimer's. The best view of it is found in a book by a nursing-home doctor named Bert Keizer. In *Dancing with Mr. D.* Keizer describes several euthanasia cases in which he provided lethal injections. In every case, he depicts the lives of frail and dying people under his care as pointless, useless, ugly, grotesque. Those with whom he interacts all seem to share these views, including his colleagues, family members of patients, and the patients themselves—allowing Keizer to kill patients without bad conscience.

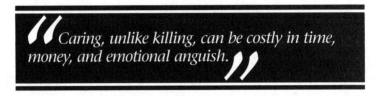

Caring, unlike killing, can be costly in time, money, and emotional anguish.

One man he describes probably has lung cancer but the diagnosis is never certain. When a colleague asks, "Why rush?" while pointing out that the man isn't suffering terribly, Keizer snaps, "Is it for us to answer this question? All I know is that he wants to die more or less upright and that he doesn't want to crawl to his grave the way a dog crawls howling to the sidewalk after he's been hit by a car."

Keizer either doesn't know or doesn't care that with proper medical treatment, people with lung cancer don't have to die in unmitigated agony. The next day, he lethally injects the patient, telling his colleagues as he walks to the man's room, "If anyone so much as whispers cortisone [a palliative agent] or 'uncertain diagnosis,' I'll hit him."

Legalized Murder

Another patient Keizer kills is disabled by Parkinson's disease. The patient requests euthanasia, but before the act can be carried out, he hesitates after receiving a letter from his religious brother who warns that God is against suicide. This upsets Keizer, who writes: "I don't know what to do with such a wavering death wish. It's getting on my nerves. Does he want to die or doesn't he? I do hope we won't have to go over the whole business again, right from the very start."

Keizer decides to push the process along. He asks the nursing-home chaplain to assure the man that his euthanasia will not upset God. The man reconsiders and again decides he wants to die. Keizer is quick with the lethal injection, happy the man has "good veins." The patient expires before his uncertainty can disturb his doctor's mood again.

Where is the compassion in this? Caring, unlike killing, can be costly in time, money, and emotional anguish. But, as the near universal outpouring of admiration for Nancy Reagan as caregiver demonstrates, it also ennobles and liberates. Indeed, as Ronald Reagan wrote long before he knew the words would apply so personally:

> My Administration is dedicated to the preservation of America as a free land, and there is no cause more important for preserving that freedom than affirming the transcendent right to life of all human beings, the right without which no other rights have any meaning.

7

Right to Die Advocates Are Undermining Democracy in America

Linda Kimball

Linda Kimball is a contributor to Sierra Times.

Social justice advocates, who claim to want fairness for all, are actually working to establish America as a communist state. The right to die movement is a part of the social justice movement. Right to die advocates falsely claim that all *Americans* have the right to "quality of life," but no such right is mentioned in the U.S. Constitution. By advocating for the right to die, these communist sympathizers are paving the way for the elimination of the elderly, the disabled, and the very poor.

"We hold these truths to be self-evident, that all men are created equal, that they are endowed by the Creator with certain inalienable Rights, that among these are Life, Liberty, and the pursuit of Happiness."—Declaration of Independence.

The preceding statement points to the Creator as the author of our Natural rights. This is the very same Creator who likewise authored the Ten Commandments (Natural Law), which place moral constraints upon our behavior in the exercising of our rights and which also serves as the moral basis to our Rule of Law.

The way it works is like this: Freedom of speech is coupled to an obligation to be respectful to others. Freedom of the press is paired with a moral duty to not bear false witness. "Thou shalt not kill. . ." speaks to the sanctity of human life, life created by God and therefore not for man to deprive his fellow man of. The second and tenth Commandments state, with respect to the judiciary: "Thou shalt not worship yourselves in any way," and "Thou shalt not covet power that belongs to the other legislative branches and to the people."

Social Justice

Certain members of SCOTUS (Supreme Court of US), along with other renegade judges and communistic ideologues, all with neither loyalty to nor belief in our traditional values and system of government, are breaking those moral laws as well as others in their pursuit of internationalism and social justice.

Social justice boils down to this dangerously insane utopianistic notion: "that 'somebody' should have the power to make life fair for everyone else". This means that "somebody" should have the power to determine what each and every individual can have or not have, which now includes whether you can still be designated as either a male or a female. It also means that "somebody" should have the power to determine if an individual's "quality of life" is such that he should go on living . . . or if he should just die.

Eliminating Differences

The end state, or desired goal of social justice is communism. According to social justice crackpots, the state of communism cannot be attained until all "social tensions" (differences) have been eliminated, hence the need for "somebody" to have complete control over everyone else. To put this into context, think of how social justice activists are currently trying to "eliminate differences" between same-sex people and heterosexuals. They're doing this by stripping documents of all references to "mother/father," "husband/wife," "grandfather/grandmother" and replacing those with gender neutral terms. They're agitating for gender-free public restrooms, conditioning children to experiment with homosexuality, waging war against traditional marriage, and even boldly proclaiming that any mention of heterosexuality is "heteronormalism." The goal of this madness is to force heterosexuals to no longer exist as such through the "elimination of differences" (causes of social tensions). Only then will they consider that social justice on behalf of homosexuals has been achieved.

It is social justice seekers who are trivializing our Constitution out of existence through the deceptive practice of "discovering" hitherto unknown "new" (bogus) rights which they call civil rights and/or human rights. Think about this, Americans: Just as there is no such thing as the "separation of church and state" clause, neither is there a Constitutional category of rights called "civil rights or human rights." These things are counterfeits.

The end state, or desired goal of social justice is communism.

But consider how they've been destroying our Constitutionally guaranteed rights and debasing our culture at the same time by bestowing these fraudulent rights on, for example, pornographers (the right to produce and market vile degradation?); on abortion mills (the right to kill the unborn?); on illegals (the right to possess drivers' licenses, collect welfare and free medical care?); on people who engage in same-sex (the right to teach our children this and to conduct lewdly sexualized parades?); on telemarketers (so they can invade our homes?); how about the "right" not to be offended by whatever might be construed as offensive at any given moment so long as it's something anchored to our traditional culture, such as Ten Commandments monuments or the Boy Scouts because they refuse to submit to the tyranny of political correctness? Or how about the latest social justice issue being discussed by animal rights activists? They want animals to have, among other things, the "Constitutional" right to own land. Next thing you know, we'll hear that social justice activists are demanding that dung beetles be awarded the Constitutional right that their "piles" never be disturbed.

The Right to Die

The "right to die," which falls under the banner of "quality of life" is yet another social justice scheme. After all, how "fair" is it that an adulterous husband have his "quality of life" be adversely affected by the burden of maintaining the life of his disabled wife?[1] That's just terribly unfair. As usual, in all social justice issues, the underlying theme is "me, myself, and I."

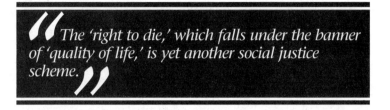

The 'right to die,' which falls under the banner of 'quality of life,' is yet another social justice scheme.

"Quality of life" [QOL] is a purposely misleading term that serves as a facade behind which lurks a multi-tentacled social theory that doesn't just concern itself with human health. It's more like an umbrella under which are social issues that concern themselves with human impact upon environment, economy, population demographics (population control, primarily), and global citizenship. All of these issues call for "elimination" of defective, surplus, and ideologically unwanted human beings.

> "There are essentially two perspectives taken in quality of life research: social indicators research which considers the . . . valuation of what people need, and conventional QOL . . . which studies what people want."—QOL, Ramkrishna Mukherjee, Sage Publications, 1989

> "The purpose of the QOL index is to provide a tool . . . which can be used to monitor key indicators that encompass social, health, environmental, and economic dimensions. . . ."—Ontario Social Development Council, 1997

Quality of Life

When, for instance, Hitler gained power he persuaded Germans to accept the "right to die" notion. Having accomplished that, the "quality of life" concept was then introduced.

From there it became a matter of eliminating the "useless eaters" and "parasites." On behalf of the "quality of life" social theory, Hitler relieved the German State of the unfair burden of

---

1. In April 2005, Terri Schiavo, a brain-damaged patient, was removed from life support at the urging of her husband.

having to care for and/or abide with 250,000 human "parasites:" retarded, institutionalized elderly who lacked family or funds, disabled, psychiatric patients, deaf, blind-welfare recipients, convicts, street people, the very poor, ideologically unwanted, religious "extremists," and anyone deemed disloyal. All of those people were "humanely" killed by starvation and/or gassing, followed by cremation. Just as is being done to Terri Schiavo, who is scheduled to be cremated as well. Megalomaniac [Soviet dictator Joseph] Stalin, not to be outdone by the likes of Hitler, also "eliminated" social tensions in his quest for social justice. His extermination program "eliminated" even more millions of humans than did Hitler's "humane holocaust".

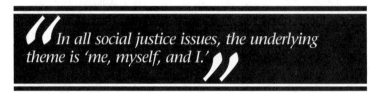

In all social justice issues, the underlying theme is 'me, myself, and I.'

I wonder if in the beginning stages of Hitler's humane holocaust whether Germans had debated the merits of their "new right," the "right to die" as Americans are doing? I wonder if among their news and political pundits there were those who sanctimoniously called the "sanctity of life" faction, "religious extremists and nuts?"

The Christian-Judeo Worldview

Our traditional Christian-Judeo worldview led to the creation of a system of government that guaranteed individual rights, equality of opportunity, a guarantee of personal property, and an inalienable right to life for every American. It also led to a common identity, and a system of moral and ethical beliefs upon which our Rule of Law is anchored and which also serves as the basis for our common culture. It gave us a "culture of life," where families and their children flourished and human beings would never be mercifully "starved to death."

More than a century ago, James Russell Lowell, Minister of State for the US to England was attending a banquet at which atheist/human secular "social justice" scoffers were heaping scorn on Christianity. Lowell said to them: "I challenge any skeptic to find a ten square mile spot on this planet where they can live their lives in peace and safety and decency, where womanhood is honored, where infancy and old age are revered, where they can educate their children, where the Gospel of Jesus Christ has not gone first to prepare the way. If they can find such a place, then I encourage them to emigrate thither and there proclaim their unbelief."

Cultural Crisis

America is not in the ever-deepening cultural crisis she is currently in because of Christian-Judeo morals and principles. She's in crisis because of a deplorable lack of them. Social justice is a genocide-inducing nightmare conceived of in evil madness and carried out in the same.

Americans . . . its imperative that we wake up before America, as we have known her, ceases to exist. We must steer a course back towards the path America was meant to be traversing; the one our founders had blazed for America. Social justice seekers are driving America onto the rocks and towards horrors heretofore unimagined.

> ". . . evil is nothing but a privation of good, which
> can continue to the point where a thing ceases to
> exist altogether"—Augustine

The hour grows late. Let us not wait till America has been drained of all her goodness.

they have demonstrated their determination to reverse any laws, legal rulings, constitutional precedents, and public opinion that may stand in their way—to recast the whole existing legal and political framework if necessary, to bring their horrific vision of righteousness into command.

Throughout these days of hysteria, they have portrayed the whole state and federal judiciary as dangerously out-of-touch, dictatorial, and anti-human—and they will exploit this as an opening shot for their coming campaign to pack the Supreme Court with extreme fascists of the [Justice Antonin] Scalia-type.

In a bizarre special session (on Palm Sunday!) an unprecedented law was passed by both the U.S. Senate and House of Representatives without any serious opposition. It tried to have this private end-of-life matter hoisted into federal courts—where, it was hoped, a federal judge might order Terri Schiavo's feeding tube reinserted. And by federal decree, everything else was supposed to be swept away: Michael Schiavo's legal rights as husband/guardian, well-established principles of constitutional federalism, the governing content of Florida state law, and 15 years of painstaking legal decisions.

And President [George W.] Bush cut his vacation short, flying into Washington to sign the bill and prance in public as part of this fascist circus.

Christian Fascists

Anyone who thinks theocracy (rule by religious fundamentalist dictatorship) is unlikely for the United States—needs to look more closely: These Christian fascist forces are *already* swaggering in the corridors of power.

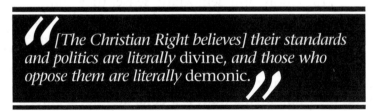

[The Christian Right believes] their standards and politics are literally divine, and those who oppose them are literally demonic.

For years, far too many people have believed that these Christian fascists are too extreme, too bizarre, too lunatic, and too backward to possibly wrap their fingers around real power in this empire. It has been widely believed that they are simply the low-level, manipulated foot soldiers of Republican business-as-usual. But this is a very dangerous underestimation of them, and of this moment.

This time, the Christian fascists were frustrated in their legal attempts to reinsert a feeding tube into Terri Schiavo. And, as we go to press, it looks like she will finally get to escape from her awful, artificially sustained limbo. [Terri Schiavo died on March 31, 2005.]

But she has not escaped from their plans to use her as a symbol. These forces will now drag the body of Terri Schiavo around inside U.S. politics—the way they have dragged bottled fetuses around outside women's clinics.

They will used this episode to color and hype the coming battles over Supreme Court justices and to prepare the ground for everything that follows.

They will use it to paint themselves as "pro-life"—and all their opponents as "pro-death."

They will use this as supposed proof that the United States needs a cultural, moral and political purge—as proof that *they* need to rule directly with a hard and merciless hand, hammering down those who resist, locking life and culture into mindless conformity and obedience. They envision a grim and theocratic America "girded" against "evil," prepared to wage and win an endless war for domination over the world, all in the name of their god.

Tom DeLay, a corrupt kingmaker of fascism's rise, has said that this struggle over Terri Schiavo was a "gift" to his allies! And that one of the great outcomes of this has been *"to elevate the visibility of what's going on in America."*

There it stands. Visible.

The Interrupted Death of Terri Schiavo

"Her CAT scan shows massive shrinkage of the brain. Her EEG is flat-flat. There's no electrical activity coming from her brain."
—Neurologist Dr. Ronald Cranford,
University of Minnesota Medical School,
examined Terri Schiavo for Florida state
courts, *New York Times*, March 23

In 1990, Terri Schiavo, then a young woman in her twenties, collapsed in her home. She had been caught up in a cycle of bulimic purges to stay slim. Her heart stopped. Oxygen was cut off from her brain. Drastic measures later revived her body, but it was too late. The great mass of her brain cells had died for lack of oxygen. Her brain stem survived and automatic body functions like breathing and circulation continued. Terri Schiavo was not literally "brain dead," but she was so severely brain damaged that she had lost any human consciousness. Many of the dead cells are so decomposed that they were described as "liquefied." Large empty spaces opened inside her skull where her cerebral cortex used to be.

For 15 years, she did not have any thoughts or emotions. She had no brain cells used to feel pain or store memory. She literally could not see or respond.

Her body was caught in restless cycles of unconscious muscle movements. But the human being Terri Schiavo was gone. This was not a coma; it was a "persistent vegetative state" and it was irreversible.

Christian fascist forces are already *swaggering in the corridors of power.*

A person cannot think without a brain. When human beings lose their brain, they cannot "just come back" to consciousness and life. Michael Schiavo explained that before her brain injury, his wife had made explicit her wishes to not be artificially kept alive without hope or real humanity. And so the decision was made to stop artificially prolonging her life. But then, the Religious Right decided to pour their activists and funds into a campaign to keep her artificially alive, coldly using the grief of Terri Schiavo's parents as a prop.

Opposing the Right to Die

In particular, they renewed and strengthened a political coalition between militantly orthodox Catholics and fundamentalist born-again Protestants in a fight to oppose the "right to die." They have worked to portray Terri Schiavo as an endangered innocent, a victim, and a symbol of the heartlessness of modern life.

And so the tragedy of Terri Schiavo's brain damage was compounded by the hysterical campaign to stop her death.

Rarely in legal history has a case been dragged through as many stages. At least 19 judges have heard the case in six courts. Before this latest round, it had already been appealed to the Supreme Court three times. There had been repeated court-ordered independent medical exams. And the results have always been the same—based on Florida law and the massive evidence, the courts ordered artificial support to be withdrawn. Three times her feeding tube had been removed—and each time, the Religious Right fought to have that reversed.

> *[The Religious Right] renewed and strengthened a political coalition between militantly orthodox Catholics and fundamentalist born-again Protestants in a fight to oppose the 'right to die.'*

Their crusade was heartless, dogmatic, ruthless and highly calculated.

Hangmen Praise Life

"In extraordinary circumstances like this, it is always wise to err on the side of life."
—President George W. Bush, March 21

"If you have more concern for a bunch of trees or beached dolphins than you do for an innocent human being, what does it say about your overall view of life?"

—Rush Limbaugh

"Why are they so committed to this woman's death? They seem to have fallen half in love with death."
—Peggy Noonan, Former Reagan speech-writer, *Wall Street Journal*, Opinion, March 24

Not for one second can these forces be allowed to masquerade as being "on the side of life."

George W. Bush is the master executioner of Texas. He is the war-maker who unleashed "shock and awe" over Baghdad. His hands drip with blood from unjust war.

The world Bush dreams of, a McWorld of unrestricted sweatshops and U.S. military dominance, would be a chamber of horrors built on human bones. You can't wave the Bible over CIA torture camps and make them into outposts of "human dignity."

And [conservative commentator] Rush Limbaugh raves about how American rightwing warrior-commandos are "doing god's work" as they rampage through mountain villages of Afghanistan [after the 2001 war there]. So much for being "on the side of life."

These forces shred the social net, casually discard the unproductive, and shove the poor and sick off the radar screen of public discussion.

And yet they pimp off the discontent of millions of people—who see that U.S. society has become even more cold and impersonal. The sense of community has evaporated—until all that remains for many people is work, family and church. And that too is deeply alienating and unsatisfying. Possession, domination, and neglect often masquerades as family and love. Work, when you've got it, is an impersonal rat race of use-and-be-used. Whole industries and towns shrivel because of the restless movement of capital. Often the most vivid human experiences in many lives all seem to involve the exchange of money. And then, as all this sickens the hearts of people, the heartless powerbrokers of a corrupt system repackage themselves as defenders of "life."

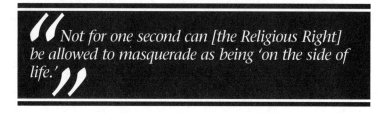

Not for one second can [the Religious Right] be allowed to masquerade as being 'on the side of life.'

They are trying to draw in public support for a dangerous lurch to the hard right. And their deceit cannot be allowed to pass unchallenged.

Raw Lies Assault Medical Truth

The Christian fascists insist their latest public crusade has been a fight to "save Terri." But the simple medical fact is that no one could "save Terri"—she was already long gone.

Always eager to bash "educated liberal elites"—the Religious Right simply mocked and rejected the clear medical evidence in this case. Often there was crude falsification: Bill Frist, the fundamentalist-surgeon-turned-Senate-leader, announced that Terri Schiavo was still "clearly responsive"—basing his long-distance diagnosis on a videotape.

In fact, the brief video clip of Terri Schiavo that everyone saw on TV had been cherry-picked from hours of footage—so her random eye movements seemed to be tracking objects, or her grimace seemed like a smile.

After the feeding tube had been pulled, Florida Governor Jeb Bush hauled a fundamentalist hack, Dr. William P. Chesire, Jr., into the limelight. Chesire babbled: "Although Terri did not demonstrate during our 90-minute visit compelling evidence of verbalization, conscious awareness or volitional behavior, yet the visitor has the distinct sense of the presence of a living human being who seems at some level to be aware of some things around her."

It was even claimed that Terri's moans over the last week [March 2005] were an attempt to communicate—and specifically an attempt to say she wanted to live. This is impossible; it was self-deception at best, and a deliberate hoax at worst.

Shameful Distortion

In a shameful distortion, the U.S. Conference of Catholic Bishops described Schiavo as "a woman with cognitive disabilities"! These Christian conservatives were claiming that this Schiavo case puts disabled people in danger of legalized execution.

But Terri Schiavo was neither disabled nor handicapped— she was in fact gone. And the truth is that this Republican Right is notoriously *indifferent* to all the real difficulties facing disabled people—including poverty, medical coverage, and the struggle for physical access.

The Christian fascist machinery claimed that a woman without a functioning brain was communicating. And they did it to portray their political opponents as cold agents of "legal murder."

It was calculated deceit.

9

Government Should Not Violate the Right to Die

Joan Ryan

Joan Ryan is a columnist for the San Francisco Chronicle.

The state of California is considering a bill to legalize physician-assisted suicide. Opponents of the bill, particularly advocacy groups for the disabled, are concerned that legalizing physician-assisted suicide would lead to involuntary euthanasia. However, the California bill is based on a similar law enacted in Oregon, which has safeguards built in to prevent abuse. The small number of terminally ill people who wish to control the time and manner of their death should be granted that right. Just as Americans do not want the government to interfere with how they live their lives, they do not want the government dictating how they will die.

Editor's Note: As this volume went to press, the California bill had not become law.

All things being equal, I will always root for more options rather than fewer. I appreciate a government that gives me the freedom to make my own decisions: where I go to school, what jobs I take, where I live, how many children I have, when and whether to marry.

I imagine most Americans are with me on this one. We want our government to let us live as we choose. So why do we stand for a government that won't let us die as we choose?

Two state legislators plan to introduce a bill this year [2005] that would make physician-assisted suicide legal in California.[1] The bill will be modeled on the law in Oregon, the only state in which assisted suicide is legal. The law applies only to terminally ill patients with less than six months to live.

Careful Safeguards

To acquire the medication necessary to bring on death, a person must get the approval of two doctors who determine that the person is mentally competent. If the physicians suspect depression, they can compel a psychiatric evaluation. The person must then make a written and oral request. After a waiting period, the doctor can write the prescription. The process generally takes about two weeks. Patients must be capable of administering the dosage themselves.

Aside from religious objections, the strongest arguments against the Oregon law [Oregon enacted the Death with Dignity act in 1997]—as now against the proposed California one —have come from disability-rights groups. Their concerns are understandable.

Why do we stand for a government that won't let us die as we choose?

"Lives of people with disabilities have historically not been valued, and any person affected by this bill is de facto a person of disability," said Deborah Doctor of Protection & Advocacy Inc., a California group that has not taken a position on the proposal yet. "It opens the door to further devaluation of the lives of people with disabilities."

Fears of the Disabled

Stephen Drake is a research analyst for Not Dead Yet, a disability-rights group based in Illinois that is mounting opposition to

1. As this volume went to press, the bill had not passed.

California's bill. He says the proposal, like Oregon's law, discriminates against the disabled. It makes suicide legal and accessible to them but not for others, in effect clearing the way for the disabled to kill themselves.

"In California and every other state, health care workers and law enforcement professionals are supposed to respond to those who want to commit suicide and stop them," Drake said. "But by allowing this one group to carry out suicide with assistance says it is less valuable than everyone else is. This is a door opener to the larger movement of euthanasia."

He said he fears families, doctors and health maintenance organizations would be given the means to end the lives of vulnerable disabled people who are considered a costly burden.

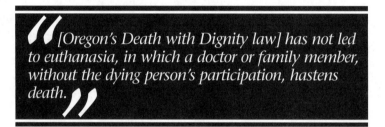

[Oregon's Death with Dignity law] has not led to euthanasia, in which a doctor or family member, without the dying person's participation, hastens death.

But doctors who treat dying patients see a great difference between those who have a fixed disability and those who have become disabled through terminal illness. In the latter, the disability is progressing. "They are clinically and morally different situations," said Dr. Robert Brody, a UCSF [University of California at San Francisco] medical professor who is also chief of the Pain Consultation Clinic and the ethics committee at San Francisco General Hospital. He has worked with Compassion in Dying, the group that pushed for the Oregon law.

He understands why disabled people might fear such a law, given the history of abuse and even demonization. "Is a disabled person vulnerable? Perhaps, but not necessarily. I think it's demeaning to say disabled people don't have the capacity or the right to make the choices others do. How is that respecting the rights of people with disabilities?"

The Oregon Experience

The experience in Oregon during the past six years is instructive, especially in assessing the legitimacy of the arguments against the California proposal. None of the doomsday predictions have come true. It has not led to euthanasia, in which a doctor or family member, without the dying person's participation, hastens death. And no person with a fixed disability has been assisted in suicide. The safeguards in the law make such an act illegal.

Shouldn't each of us decide for ourselves what makes life worth living?

From 1998 through 2003, just 171 people in Oregon ended their lives through physician-assisted suicide. Eighty-eight percent were 55 or older. Many who acquired the medication never used it but said they were comforted by having the option readily available. The reasons patients gave for seeking assisted suicide were similar: Most said they wanted to end their lives because they had lost their autonomy, could no longer engage in activities that made life enjoyable, and feared losing their dignity.

Many in the disabled community understandably take offense at this last reason. Many disabled people live their entire lives with such so-called indignities and still find life worth living. But shouldn't each of us decide for ourselves what makes life worth living? Should my standard be forced on you or yours on me?

Prisoners of Technology

"We all die," said Dr. Steven Pantilat, director of the Palliative Care Service at UCSF. He teaches a course on end-of-life care at the university. "The way we die in America is often very different from the way we want to die. We can do it better, giving people meaningful time with their families, allowing them to be at home. But most end up prisoners of technology."

Pantilat said one or two patients a year ask him to help hasten their deaths. He always asks, "Why are you bringing this up today?" He listens to their fears, and in almost every case, the requests go away when they are assured their pain can be managed and that they can be cared for with dignity.

"Good palliative care can take care of most of the fears people have about dying," he said, making note of the tiny percentage of people in Oregon who have made use of the law. Still, with safeguards in place, he supports assisted suicide for those few people who feel strongly about being in control of their deaths. In California now, such people cannot be with family and friends in those final moments; aiding and abetting a suicide is illegal.

We recognize that we have different values and live in different circumstances from each other, and we make individual decisions that reflect those variables. We don't want the government telling us how to live our lives. Why, then, do we tolerate it telling us how to end them?

10

Granting People the Right to Die Ignores Their Responsibilities to Society

Fred Hutchison

Fred Hutchison is the author of The Stages of Sanctification, *which examines spiritual maturity from a Christian perspective.*

Proponents of the right to die believe that people should be in complete control of their own lives, which includes making decisions without considering their impact on society. Even though allowing people to choose to die would inevitably lead to involuntary euthanasia and a general decline in the value of human life, right to die advocates staunchly defend an individual's right to choose death. This immoral stance emerged from the philosophy of existentialism, which advocates absolute freedom. Existentialism in the 1960s led to the sexual revolution, which in turn led to legalized abortion. The right to slaughter unborn babies has now produced the right to kill disabled people by drugging them or removing feeding tubes.

By coincidence, both Terri Schiavo [a brain-damaged woman whose husband successfully sought to disconnect her from a feeding tube] and Pope John Paul II, the great advocate of the value of life, had feeding tubes inserted by doctors. Both Terri and the pope evidenced the desire to live: Terri did so by her sunny attitudes, and the pope did so by his writings about the sanctity of life.

The difference was that Terri was not dying, nor did she have control of events. The aged pope was dying, but could dictate what his health care should be.

Terri's feeding tube was pulled out in spite of her apparent desire to live, and she died according to the will of others. It was a painful death in spite of all the denials. The pope died at the time decreed by divine providence. He was peaceful at the end and his last word was "amen," meaning "so be it," as though he was accepting a visit of the death angel. He agreed with death when it came, but he did not arrange for its early arrival. He agreed with life until the appointed time of his departure from his mortal body.

Deciding the Hour of Death

Do we have the right to decide the hour of our death, or do we have the duty to live until the death angel comes for us? Is heaven the rightful arbiter of life and death, or do men have the right to take such matters into their own hands?

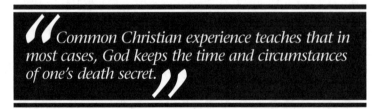

Common Christian experience teaches that in most cases, God keeps the time and circumstances of one's death secret.

Common Christian experience teaches that in most cases, God keeps the time and circumstances of one's death secret, as though this information is something that trembling fragile mortals cannot handle. Yet a large, influential minority of the population believes that the individual should have the right to determine the time and means of his death, once he decides that life is not worth living.

But is there any such thing as a "life not worth living?" Are not these code words that mean, "I lack the moral courage to face certain kinds of suffering?" Or do they mean, "I refuse to be humbled, lose control and be reduced to a dependent state?"

Of course, the pride one refuses to surrender is partly an illusion. The control that some folks cannot bear to yield is partly an illusion. Many people can change aspects of their mode of living, and some can have a significant influence upon the world if they mean to have it, but mere mortals have no control of outcomes.

The Illusion of Control

"The best laid plans of mice and men gang aft agley" (Robert Burns). (The best plans go askew.) Translations of Scottish dialect invariably water down the color and force of idiomatic expressions. "Gang aft agley" might signify to a man with Scottish peasant roots like Burns, a practical disaster. Picture Burns carefully steering a cart down a hill on a country lane. The cart picks up speed, breaks away, and runs "gang aft agley" off the road and crashes into a stone wall. A smart plan, good strong arm, and fixed will cannot insure against unexpectedly bad outcomes.

Doctors were certain that Terri would not suffer, but she suffered anyway. The carefully steered cart went off the road and crashed. We cannot control outcomes, and our myopic eyes blur and our clumsy hands fumble when we try to manipulate the delicate process of dying.

In Shakespeare's *Romeo and Juliet*, Juliet took a potion that simulated death to escape an arranged marriage and then, with assistance, planned to sneak out of the tomb and elope with Romeo. The plan went awry because Romeo failed to receive the message that explained the plan. He discovered Juliet ostensibly dead in the tomb and killed himself. She awakened to find him laying dead next to her and killed herself. Disaster leads to disaster.

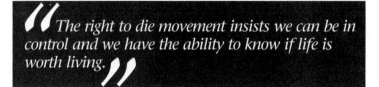

The right to die movement insists we can be in control and we have the ability to know if life is worth living.

The classical Greeks understood that the hero can perform wondrous exploits, but only the gods can control destiny. If the hero was destined by the gods to doom, he was accounted noble if he behaved himself virtuously, fought his appointed battles, and displayed manly fortitude and insouciant flair as he calmly sailed with resignation into the jaws of inescapable death. The Greek heroes went to their doom with style, much like British gentlemen of a prior century who would tell dry jokes and puns on their way to the gallows.

The pope was as dry as an Englishman during his last days. He was asked how he felt during a time when he was wracked with pain. As a man calmly reconciled to his death, he responded with dry insouciance, "Below the neck, not so good." (I.e., I am fine, but this donkey of a body has gang aft agley.)

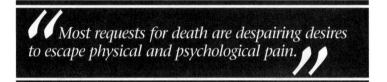

Most requests for death are despairing desires to escape physical and psychological pain.

In contrast to the Greek, English, and papal model, the European tragic literature is fatalistic, for the hero had a hand in bringing himself down. In spite of all his virtues, powers, and victories, he is defeated in the end by a fatal flaw in character. For all his powers to bring change to the world and all his cleverness to manipulate events, he cannot stage-manage the outcome of his personal story. Despite all his influence upon events, the world spins off in directions he never imagined. Faust and MacBeth were tragedies of this kind.

A Life Worth Living

The right to die movement insists we can be in control and we have the ability to know if life is worth living. Can we know when life is not worth living? Interestingly, the demand for Dr. [Jack] Kevorkian's [a physician who helped several people commit suicide] assisted suicides declined sharply when doctors started to aggressively treat chronic pain in the elderly, physically afflicted, and depressed. This medical revolution involves prescription drugs to aggressively relieve physical pain, and more subtle treatments of drugs and counseling to relieve the psychological pain of depression. Most requests for death are despairing desires to escape physical and psychological pain. Once the pain is relieved through medical treatment, the innate desire to live returns in most cases and thoughts of calling Dr. Death [i.e., Kevorkian] for assisted suicide are put away.

An investigation of the capers of Dr. Death might reveal some carts that have gang aft agley. Some folks are astonishingly difficult to kill. Murder is messy, and the Hollywood image of the hit man who administers a quick, clean, efficient death is a myth. The fastest way to disillusion a woman's right to choose advocate is to have her watch an abortion and to supply her with a barf bag in case she becomes ill. Life is beautiful, and murder is ugly. Death by enforced dehydration and starvation, as Terri Schiavo suffered, is one of the ugliest.

The pope was in great pain but did not seek death because he had spiritual hope and believed that pain can play a role in the sanctification process. Spiritual hope reinforces the innate desire to live, and spiritual duty engenders a commitment to complete the earthly journey assigned according to providential design, and to endure fiery ordeals in trust and surrender.

As for estimating what a "life worth living" might be, is any mortal being capable of understanding the mystery of life, much less able to evaluate the worthiness of a life? Such assessments are invariably made on shallow grounds, such as whether a person feels happy or useful.

A feeling of liberation and new wisdom often comes with the realization that life does not necessarily have to have happy feelings or be useful in a utilitarian sense. Life is innately good apart from such calculations. The Creator has priorities for life that go far beyond transitory feelings and practical functions. Feelings and functions are the surface froth of a deep ocean. A spiritually and intellectually shallow society is easily seduced by spurious and superficial values based upon the surface froth of life and may lapse into a dysfunctional code of morality.

Why did the Terri Schiavo case center around the question of what Terri would have wanted before her brain damage if she knew what was ahead? From whence comes the assumption that a person should be allowed to commit suicide if they want to? If we recall the Existentialist revolution of the 1950's and sixties, some of the answers come clear.

The Existentialist Revolution

Americans have valued free will and personal autonomy since the founding of the republic. However, prior generations did not necessarily associate the act of choosing with virtue or being in the right. After all, one may freely choose vice, perversion, and criminality. The freely chosen course of action must be moral and wise to be worthy of commendation.

The philosophy of Existentialism places the emphasis on the mode of choosing instead of the intended outcomes of the choice. It places the value upon subjective questions such as whether the choice was really free—independent of pressures to conform—and whether the person is committed to his choice. What matters to Existentialists is whether one's choices are "authentic" and "sincere."

These are indeed interesting questions.

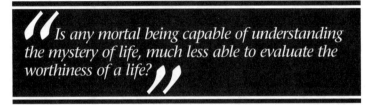

Is any mortal being capable of understanding the mystery of life, much less able to evaluate the worthiness of a life?

But if these are the only questions we ask, we may never get around to considering whether the outcomes of our decisions are wise, prudent, responsible, and edifying to our families and our communities. If others get hurt by our choices, it is easy to evade responsibility if we look at the freedom of the will as the highest arbiter. "Let my will be done though the heavens fall." This is a deliberate misquote of [eighteen-century British judge] Lord Mansfield's famous saying concerning a slavery trial, "Let justice be done though the heavens fall." Existentialism replaces justice with free will as the highest imperative. When free will becomes an end in itself, the moral law is brushed aside. The universal moral law exists so that the man should learn to live within boundaries and rein in his will, so that freedom is a blessing and not a curse.

Existentialism and Commitment

The philosophy of Existentialism has gone through a complex and tangled development since the time of [Danish philosopher] Soren Kierkegaard (1813–1855), who invented a Christian Existentialism of sorts. The form of Existentialism that influenced American culture in the 1950's and 60's was the atheistic French Existentialism promoted by [French philosopher] Jean-Paul Sartre (1905–1980) and [French writer] Albert Camus (1913–1960). Sartre and Camus rejected the universal moral law and values imposed by society.

Sartre insisted that human existence is always individual

and particular. It is always a case of my existence and your existence, and the two are radically separate as though each of us lives sealed in a morally air tight world. Sartre defined existence as a mode of being. The way one chooses to live is his particular mode of being. As the individual chooses from a wide range of possibilities and commits himself to those choices, he defines his existence.

What is important to Sartre is not which choices are made, but how they are made. What matters is whether the choices are made with commitment and sincerity, and whether one chooses with absolute freedom, that is to say, freedom from guile, from the conformist opinions of others, from the values of society, and any notion of a transcendent realm or a universal moral law.

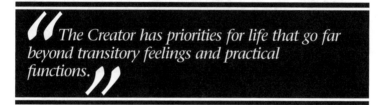

The Creator has priorities for life that go far beyond transitory feelings and practical functions.

An Existentialist can be hard as nails in sticking to his choices once he convinces himself he chose freely, sincerely, and with commitment. If someone condemns his choice based upon a higher moral law, he will be outraged. The Existentialist is convinced that he has the right to contrive a private moral world all of his own, and any challenge to that private world is a moral outrage and a threat to freedom. These folks are in earnest and they are not playing games—to the extent they are real Existentialists, and not mere hypocrites playing Existentialist games to rationalize misbehavior. The two kinds are hard to tell apart, of course.

Authenticity

What do Existentialists mean when they speak about commitment? They often mean sticking with a decision and not worrying overmuch about the outcomes. Sincerity in the decision and commitment to the decision are tests of "authenticity."

One has an authentic existence if he chooses his mode of life with sincerity and commitment. Does commitment mean taking responsibility for one's actions? In the sense of standing up for one's decisions, yes. In the sense of taking responsibility for the harm one's actions cause others, maybe not. A nihilism and antisocial streak runs through the writings of Sartre and Camus.

Once one severs the links with the universal moral law and with obligations to society, sliding down the slippery slope towards narcissism, nihilism, and irresponsible behavior are almost inevitable. Sartre himself slid down that slope. He sat through World War II in Paris sidewalk cafes jotting notes about his philosophical ideas. Kierkegaard would have regarded that as inauthentic, irresponsible, and unaware behavior, and sins against Existentialist ideals.

> *The Existentialist is convinced that he has the right to contrive a private moral world all his own, and any challenge to that private world is a moral outrage and a threat to freedom.*

During the sixties, Sartre demonstrated his "commitment" by becoming a quasi-Marxist and visiting college campuses and egging on the rioting students to revolution. The economic determinism, utopian ideals, and socialist theory of Marxism meant nothing to Sartre. Communist totalitarian socialist systems are the very nemesis of the radical freedom of Existentialism. The essential thing to Sartre was active commitment to a movement that defies the "system" and its conformist values.

But to overthrow a system that upholds human rights and the freedom to be an Existentialist is irresponsible. Sartre slipped far from taking responsibility for the potential outcomes of his actions. If Sartre was capable of such cosmic irresponsibility, how likely is it that he would take responsibility for a wrong done to his neighbor? Existentialism is strong on the rights of freedom, but is weak on the responsibility of the citizen. . . .

The Sexual Revolution and Abortion

Existentialism on the campus—devoted to carpe diem (seize the day), and indifferent to consequences—swiftly led to a sexual revolution in academia in the late sixties. The infection spread to the general culture in the seventies. It was greatly aided by pop psychology that promoted "self esteem," "self actualization," and "taking control of your life." Soon, just as the sexual revolution was in transition from campus to general culture, abortion became a major issue and was hastily placed into law by liberal-minded judges.

Planned Parenthood vs. Casey (1992) reveals that a majority of the court supports Existentialist values concerning abortion. Justice Anthony Kennedy wrote in his opinion, "At the heart of liberty is the right to define one's own concept of existence, of meaning, of the universe, and the mystery of life." These words are pure Existentialism and could have been written by Sartre or Camus.

Defining one's own mode of existence is the very heart of the Existentialist project. However, not only is the personal mode of living to be self-defined, the universe and life itself are to be self-defined. If all men invent their own private universe, how can society exist? For that matter, how can a family or a community exist? If one is free to concoct a private definition of life, how can murder be contained? The murderer can claim that his victim did not deserve to live because he was not living an authentic life. Justice Kennedy's Existential line is a code for nihilism, anarchy, and violence.

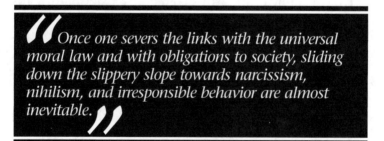

Once one severs the links with the universal moral law and with obligations to society, sliding down the slippery slope towards narcissism, nihilism, and irresponsible behavior are almost inevitable.

The culture of abortion is Existentialist in its values. A woman's "right to choose" was contrasted by the feminists with the "bondage" of the old days, when women were hemmed in with responsibilities to others. Nothing less than radical Existentialist freedom would do for the new liberated woman. Even the idea that actions have consequences must not interfere with absolute freedom. If a woman chose sex for purposes of "self actualization," no consequences like pregnancy must block the way. The impediment must be removed because achieving a free personhood of Existential authenticity is all that really matters.

The hermetically sealed narcissism of Existentialism makes

it easy to look at the babe in the womb as a hunk of protoplasm that is part of the woman's body. As long as the baby is regarded as a possession of the mother and not a body, soul, and life in its own right, the shadow of Existentialism will hang over the land.

Sexual promiscuity, Existentialist style, and the shattered family will bring infinite injury to this unhappy land. When each person is seeking absolute freedom of the will as the highest virtue, there is no place left for the fidelity and responsibility of family life.

Dismal Conclusions

After a holocaust of forty million aborted babies, the right to slaughter the innocent has been established in our laws and mores. The right to kill a baby in the womb has been extended to the right to kill a helpless person by removing her food and water. This was recently sustained by the Existentialist courts, of course.

When each man becomes like a god and does what is right in his own eyes, the earth is filled with violence. (See Genesis 6:5, 11.) The radical atheism of French Existentialism insists upon absolute freedom, creating itself, by itself, thus assuming to itself the function of God. [Christian author and philosopher] C.S. Lewis said, "When love becomes a god, it turns into a devil." Following this line of thought, when free will becomes a god, it turns into an agency for evil. At this point, we have dug down to the very core of the culture war. Our most urgent mission is to convince the American people that although free will is potentially good within limits, it is not a god.

Madame de Pompadour, mistress of Louis XV, had a premonition of the French Revolution and said, "Apres nous, le deluge." (After us, the deluge.) If we fail to convince our world that Justice Kennedy is wrong and that free will is not a god, then it may yet be that after *Planned Parenthood vs. Casey* will come the deluge.

11

People Should Have the Right to Die with Dignity

Cindy Richards

Cindy Richards has been a professional journalist in Chicago for twenty years. She has worked for both the Chicago Tribune *and* Chicago Sun-Times.

Modern technology has enabled medical personnel to prolong life, but people should be allowed the right to die a dignified death. The death of Terri Schiavo (whose feeding tube was removed at her husband's request) should prompt Americans to talk with their families about how they wish to die. Instead, the Religious Right has exploited the tragedy to argue for life at all costs.

When you think about how you want to die—and if there is anyone who hasn't thought about it in the wake of the Terri Schiavo tragedy, I'd like to hear from that person—how do you picture it?

Are you an elderly grandmother lying in your own bed surrounded by the loving faces of your children, grandchildren and great-grandchildren as you drift off into the Great Beyond?

Are you flying down the road on your motorcycle, sans helmet, challenging the fates?

Or are you lying in a nursing home, unable to care for yourself in even the most basic of ways while doctors insert or remove your feeding tube and people who love you fight over what's best for you, using lawyers, politicians and public opinion as their weapons of choice?

It's no contest for me. I choose to be that old lady who has lived a full, healthy and independent life right up to the end. And then I hope I have the courage to say to my loving family and all the doctors in a very sassy voice: "Thanks for the offer, but I think I'll pass on that heart surgery. After all, I am 85. I'll just take what comes."

Death with Dignity

That idea—that we can die a dignified death—has been lost somewhere along the way in our rush to operate and medicate and preserve a life that I would argue isn't a life at all.

I know that strikes terror in the hearts of disabled people everywhere, many of whom are living lives to the fullest of their abilities. But—excuse me for saying so—I might have made the same choice as Maggie Fitzgerald, the injured boxer at the heart of the controversial Clint Eastwood movie, "Million Dollar Baby [in which the paralyzed Maggie asks to be euthanized]."

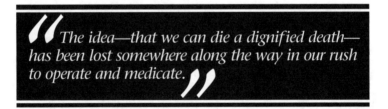

The idea—that we can die a dignified death—has been lost somewhere along the way in our rush to operate and medicate.

In our world, a world where there simply aren't enough health care dollars to go around, why aren't we talking more about ensuring death with dignity and less about prolonging life unnecessarily?

If Schiavo lived in Oregon and she had been diagnosed with a fatal disease, she might have chosen to take advantage of that state's "Death with Dignity" law. This physician-assisted suicide law would have allowed her to obtain a prescription for a lethal drug that would hasten her end and lessen her suffering.

Of course, Schiavo lives in Florida, and her incapacitation came on suddenly. That means her husband and her parents are left to make those horrendous choices (although I believe that once a child has moved on and chosen to share life with a spouse or significant other, it is that significant other, not the parents, who should have the final say).

Prolonging Life at All Costs

Because of our remarkable advances in medical technology and our cultural belief in trying to prolong life at all costs—whether in an infant born severely prematurely, a teen horribly mangled in a car accident or a senior citizen with a failing heart—there is hardly a family left in America that hasn't faced these difficult decisions.

And, the sad fact is that, despite the living wills and long conversations that (I hope) we all have had as Terri Schiavo lay dying, someone still has to make a decision to pull the plug or remove the feeding tube or turn off the ventilator.

When that decision has to be made, it's entirely reasonable to see hope where there is none. A movement that to a doctor is an involuntary muscle twitch is a sign of caution to desperate family members: She moved, therefore she might be waking up. If she is and I have agreed to remove the feeding tube, does that mean I have killed her?

I am sad that Terri's tragedy has been co-opted by the religious right who seem to believe in life at all costs (which I find to be an interesting perspective for religious Christian zealots in comparison with their Muslim counterparts who blow themselves up in search of the greater glory of the Great Beyond).

Her life could have served a much greater good. It could have served as the basis for an entirely new discussion in America, a discussion about the acceptance of death.

12

The Right to Die Will Lead to the Duty to Die

Elizabeth Nickson

Elizabeth Nickson is a columnist for the National Post.

The right to die will evolve into a duty to die. As euthanasia becomes more accepted, those who are seriously ill or disabled will be expected to choose it to relieve their families, provide replacement organs for healthy people, and cut medical costs. Many bioethicists are now redefining personhood to justify the killing of the aged, infirm, and disabled. Legalized assisted suicide and euthanasia will lead to the abuse and neglect of the elderly.

Perhaps the culture of death my generation has unwittingly created will only come home to roost when, in our creaky 80s, we face the Futile Care Committee at our local hospital, to be told, well, it's simply too expensive to keep you alive any longer, buster. Inappropriate Care Protocols rule.

Say your prayers, and your goodbyes, the lady with the "Aussie Exit Bag" [a specially designed bag to assist in suicide.] is coming, next Tuesday at 11 o'clock. Death with Dignity. Good of the State. Here's the extension of the Therapeutic Grieving Committee. You can have whatever music you want. '70s? '80s? 60s? My, you are old. And by the way? We're feeling particularly compassionate this morning.

How likely is this? Pretty much inevitable. Thirty more years of federal Liberal health care mismanagement will make it necessary. The drugs for assisted suicide cost about $40. As

Derek Humphrey, co-founder of the Hemlock Society [a right-to-die advocacy group], wrote, in his recent *Freedom to Die*, "the hastened demise of people with only a short time to live would free resources for others," an amount he predicts would run into the "hundreds of billions of dollars." That'll sure help with our ever-yawning debt.

It's unpleasant to think of, I know. And so what, right? We already see life and death through a utilitarian prism. In Canada, where only a few are willing to discuss our failing medical system, we have to be modern. We've spent our way into it.

We already see life and death through a utilitarian prism.

This was all thrown into relief this week by our [Canadian] Senate about to allow experiments on human embryos, and the U.S. Senate's finally banning partial birth abortion. Parental notification will be next, promised Bill Frist, U.S. Senate leader. After that, murdering the mother and child in utero will be two murders, not one. Then, late last week [October 2003], [Florida governor] Jeb Bush overturned the forced removal of young Floridian Terri Schiavo's feeding tube, allowing her parents another shot at taking care of her. The ACLU [American Civil Liberties Union] hooted and hollered, but most people looked at Terri's wide-boy husband spouting platitudes on [current-events television program] *Larry King* about Terri saying she wanted to die when she was watching a movie once, and thought, this guy wants to go off and play happy families with his two kids by his new girlfriend and forget all this nuisance of feeding tubes and visits. If her parents want her to live, let her live. If there's a chance, a tiny chance, that with rehab, she can eat by herself, let her be fed. When in doubt, choose life.

Schiavo's life could be richer than that. Scientists, like neuropsychologist Joseph Giancino, believe that, within ten years, researchers will be able to experiment with implanted electrodes that act like pacemakers for consciousness. By emitting regular pulses of electricity, they could keep the brain's networks active and synchronized. Terri Schiavo is a young woman, within 20 years, she could live at home, have a life. Who knows? If it's possible, even a tiny chance, science turning up one miracle after another, as it does, who would take that life away?

Defining Personhood

Well the community of bioethicists for one. This relatively new group of academics have taken it upon themselves to advise the good and the great on what life is and should be, and they are certainly behind any legislation having to do with the definition of death. Most famous among them is Princeton's Pete Singer—so mainstream he wrote the essay on ethics for the *Encyclopedia Britannica*—who argues that parents should have the right for a set period of time after each child's birth, whether to kill the child or not. "The wrongness of killing such beings [infants]," says Singer, "is not as great as the wrongness of killing a person."

What counts morally is not being "human" but being a "person," a status earned by possessing identifiable mental capabilities such as being self-aware or having the ability to engage in rational behaviour.

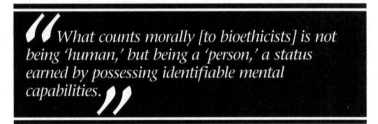

What counts morally [to bioethicists] is not being 'human,' but being a 'person,' a status earned by possessing identifiable mental capabilities.

Most bioethicists agree that there are human beings who are not persons and many bioethicists believe that basing moral value and legal rights solely upon being human is capricious, religion-based and irrational. Who doesn't cut it? All embryos, people with Alzheimer's, serious cognitive disorders, and significant developmental incapacities. Needless to say, Not Dead Yet, the disability rights group that fights against legalized assisted suicide, believes that this theory is a dagger blade aimed at the heart of the disabled community.

The Duty to Die

Personhood theory is well entrenched in the medical establishment, particularly among those transplant professionals who want to redefine death to include a diagnosis of permanent coma or unconsciousness. The thousands of people in such states, at any one time, transplant professionals argue, could have non-essential items like corneas or a single kidney removed. *The Pittsburgh Gazette* reported last year [2002] that "obitiatry," defined by Dr. [Jack] Kervorkian [a doctor who helped many people commit suicide] as experimentation on assisted suicide victims, has already been used on catastrophically ill or injured people with experimental cancer drugs. Last year, in Oregon, where assisted suicide is legal, the HMO Kaiser/Permanente solicited their doctors for physicians willing to kill patients that their own physicians refused to kill.

You have to be thinking about money now. Medical and bioethics journals have reported in recent years that futile care protocols have been adopted quietly by hospitals all over the world. Doctors can decide that given finite resources, life-sustaining treatments, even low-tech antibiotics, can be withdrawn.

And money is where the culture of death comes home to roost. As Wesley J. Smith, author of *Forced Exit*, points out, legalized assisted suicide and euthanasia will take place in the "context of a harsher real world of abuse and neglect of the elderly, family dysfunction, relatives demanding to inherit property or collect fat insurance policies and subtle pressure on the ill, disabled or elderly to cease being a burden." You can choose to die with "dignity." At the price of thousands who will be forced into it.

Organizations to Contact

The editors have compiled the following list of organizations concerned with the issues debated in this book. The descriptions are derived from materials provided by the organizations. All have publications or information available for interested readers. The list was compiled on the date of publication of the present volume; names, addresses, phone and fax numbers, and e-mail and Internet addresses may change. Be aware that many organizations take several weeks or longer to respond to inquiries, so allow as much time as possible.

American Foundation for Suicide Prevention (AFSP)
120 Wall St., 22nd Fl., New York, NY 10005
(212) 363-3500 • fax: (212) 363-6237
e-mail: inquiry@afsp.org • Web site: www.afsp.org

The American Foundation for Suicide Prevention is dedicated to advancing knowledge about suicide and society's ability to prevent it. It is the only national not-for-profit organization exclusively dedicated to funding research, developing prevention initiatives, and offering educational programs and conferences for survivors, mental health professionals, physicians, and the public. The foundation's activities include supporting research projects that help further the understanding and treatment of depression and the prevention of suicide, providing information and education about depression and suicide, and promoting professional education for the recognition and treatment of depressed and suicidal individuals. AFSP's quarterly newsletter *Lifesavers* is sent to over twenty-five hundred mental health professionals, survivors of suicide, friends, and supporters across the country.

Citizens United Resisting Euthanasia (CURE)
303 Truman St., Berkeley Springs, WV 25411
(304) 258-5433
e-mail: cureltd@verizon.net • Web site: mysite.verizon.net

Founded in 1981, CURE comprises an international grassroots network of patient-advocates from a wide range of professional, political, and religious backgrounds bound together in a common cause: uncompromising opposition to euthanasia. To this end, CURE promotes Compassion, Unity, Research, and Education. CURE's "Life Matters" brochures, "Vital Signs" columns, and a variety of other articles and reports are available on its Web site.

Compassion in Dying Federation
6312 SW Capitol Hwy. No. 415, Portland, Oregon 97239
(503) 221-9556 • fax: (503) 228-9160
e-mail: info@compassionandchoices.org
Web site: www.compassionindying.org

The Compassion in Dying Federation provides national leadership for client service, legal advocacy, and public education to improve pain and symptom management, increase patient empowerment and self-determination, and expand end-of-life choices to include aid-in-dying for terminally ill, mentally competent adults. It reaches the public through print, radio, and other broadcast media to inform people of the options at the end of life. The archives of its newsletter *Connections* as well as other publications, are available on its Web site.

Death with Dignity National Center (DDNC)
520 SW Sixth Ave., Suite 1030, Portland, OR 97204
(503) 228-4415 • fax: (503) 228-7454
e-mail: info@deathwithdignity.org
Web site: www.deathwithdignity.org

The Death with Dignity National Center has successfully proposed, passed, defended, and helped implement Oregon's first-in-the-nation law allowing terminally ill individuals meeting stringent safeguards to hasten their own deaths. Since the law's implementation, few have used it, and all were in extreme cases of late-stage terminal illness. Facts, statistics, and case stories are available on its Web site.

Disability Rights Education and Defense Fund (DREDF)
2212 Sixth St., Berkeley, CA 94710
(510) 644-2555 • fax: (510) 841-8645
e-mail: dredf@dredf.org • Web site: www.dredf.org

The Disability Rights Education and Defense Fund is the leading national law and policy center in disability rights. DREDF was founded in 1979 by a unique alliance of adults with disabilities and parents of children with disabilities. DREDF's name was chosen to align the organization with the tradition of other civil rights legal defense funds. The archives of its newsletter *Highlights* as well as press releases, articles, and other publications are available on its Web site.

Dying With Dignity
55 Eglinton Ave. East, Suite 802, Toronto, ON M4P 1G8 Canada
(416) 486-3998 • fax: (416) 486-5562
e-mail: info@dyingwithdignity.ca
Web site: www.dyingwithdignity.ca

Dying With Dignity is a charitable organization whose mission is to improve the quality of dying for all Canadians in accordance with their own wishes, values, and beliefs. It informs and educates individuals about their rights to determine and choose health care options at the end of life, provides counseling and advocacy services to members, builds public support for legal change to permit voluntary, physician-assisted suicide, and provides living wills, enduring powers of attorney for personal care, and other advance health care directives. A variety of articles and links are available on its Web site.

Embracing Our Dying
1119 K St., 2nd Fl., Sacramento, CA 95814
(916) 443-4851 • fax: (916) 443-5629
e-mail: comments@embracingourdying.com.
Web site: www.embracingourdying.com

Embracing Our Dying is a Catholic response to the political and social efforts to promote the acceptance and eventual legalization of assisted suicide in California. Included on its Web site is an overview of Catholic moral theology on death and dying, current medical and hospital practices, the state of the law regarding end-of-life issues, comments on the current political situation, and information on parish nurses, parish health ministry, hospice care, and other parish-based services.

End-of-Life Choices
PO Box 101810, Denver, CO 80250-1810
(800) 247-7421 • fax: (303) 639-1224
e-mail: info@endoflifechoices.org
Web site: www.endoflifechoices.org

Founded as the Hemlock Society in 1980, End-of-Life Choices has one core goal: to assure freedom of choice at the end of life. It advocates for the right of terminally ill, mentally competent adults to hasten death under careful safeguards. It believes that each person is entitled to choose within the law how he or she lives and dies. End-of-Life Choices has three main avenues to accomplish its goals: advocacy, education, and service. It creates, promotes, and supports legislation to maximize end-of-life options throughout the United States. Its Web site contains useful materials and links for anyone interested in the choice-in-dying movement, as well as copies of recent media releases and a complete media kit.

Euthanasia Research and Guidance Organization (ERGO)
24829 Norris Ln., Junction City, OR 97448-9559
fax: (541) 998-1873 • e-mail: ergo@efn.org
Web site: www.finalexit.org

The Euthanasia Research and Guidance Organization is a nonprofit educational corporation based in Oregon. It was founded in 1993 to improve the quality of research into assisted dying for persons who are terminally or hopelessly ill and wish to end their suffering. ERGO holds that voluntary euthanasia, physician-assisted suicide, and self-deliverance are all appropriate life endings depending on the individual, medical, and ethical circumstances. Essays, films, videos, and books are available on its Web site.

Final Exit Network
PO Box 965005, Marietta, GA 30066
(800) 524-3948
e-mail: info@finalexitnetwork.org
Web site: www.finalexitnetwork.org

The mission of the Final Exit Network is to serve people who are suffering intolerably from an incurable physical condition. The organization fosters research to find new peaceful and reliable ways to end life, promotes the use of advance directives with a durable power of attorney for health care, and advocates for individuals when their advance directives are not being honored.

International Task Force on Euthanasia and Assisted Suicide
PO Box 760, Steubenville, OH 43952
(740) 282-3810
Web site: www.internationaltaskforce.org

The International Task Force on Euthanasia and Assisted Suicide addresses the issues of euthanasia, assisted suicide, advance directives, assisted-suicide proposals, right-to-die cases, euthanasia practices in the Netherlands, disability rights, and pain control. A variety of fact sheets and articles are available on its Web site.

Living/Dying Project
PO Box 357, Fairfax, CA 94978
(415) 456-3915
e-mail: info@livingdying.org • Web site: www.livingdying.org

The Living/Dying Project was founded in 1977 and is the outgrowth of the Hanuman Foundation Dying Center in Santa Fe, New Mexico. The Living/Dying Project has been offering services in the San Francisco Bay Area since 1987. Educational services and training are available nationwide and internationally to health care providers and the general public. It brings a spiritual approach to grief and death in the hope of expanding the understanding of life-threatening illness to include the possibility of spiritual awakening, transformation, and freedom. The *Living/Dying Project Newsletter* and a variety of articles are available on its Web site.

National Right to Life Committee
512 Tenth St. NW, Washington, DC 20004
(202) 626-8800
e-mail: nrlc@nrlc.org • Web site: www.nrlc.org

The National Right to Life Committee was founded in 1973 in response to the legalization of human abortion. The primary interest of the National Right to Life Committee and its members has been the abortion controversy; however, it is also concerned with related matters of medical ethics that relate to the right-to-life issues of euthanasia and infanticide. A large variety of articles and news links can be found on its Web site.

Not Dead Yet (NDY)
7521 Madison St., Forest Park, IL 60130
(708) 209-1500 • fax: (708) 209-1735
e-mail: ndycoleman@aol.com • Web site: www.notdeadyet.org

Not Dead Yet was founded on April 27, 1996, shortly after doctor Jack Kevorkian was acquitted in the assisted suicides of two women with nonterminal disabilities. In a 1997 Supreme Court rally, the outcry of five hundred people with disabilities chanting "Not Dead Yet" was heard around the world. Since then, eleven other national disability rights groups have joined NDY in opposing legalized assisted suicide and euthanasia. Fact sheets, links, and news are available on its Web site.

Right to Die Society of Canada
145 Macdonell Ave., Toronto, ON M6R 2A4 Canada
(416) 535-0690 • fax: (416) 530-0243

The Right to Die Society of Canada was founded in 1991. Euthanasia and assisted suicide are covert and unregulated in Canada today. The Right to Die Society of Canada works to make euthanasia and assisted suicide available to all within an open, regulated, and equitable system. It publishes the magazine *Last Rights*.

Voluntary Euthanasia Society (VES)
13 Prince of Wales Terr., London, England W85 PG
44 20-7937-7770 • fax: 44 20-7376-2648
e-mail: info@ves.org.uk • Web site: www.ves.org.uk

VES promotes greater patient choice at the end of life. It is the leading supplier of living wills in the United Kingdom and campaigns for people with terminal illnesses to be allowed to ask for medical help to die at a time of their choosing within proper legal safeguards. Its Web site contains a variety of press releases, position papers, and articles.

Bibliography

Books

Ira Byock — *Dying Well: Peace and Possibilities at the End of Life.* New York: Riverhead Trade, 1998.

Raphael Cohen-Almagor — *Right to Die with Dignity: An Argument in Ethics, Medicine and Law.* Piscataway, NJ: Rutgers University Press, 2001.

Ian J. Dowbiggin — *A Concise History of Euthanasia: Life, Death, God, and Medicine.* Lanham, MD: Rowman & Littlefield, 2005.

William Dudley, ed. — *Euthanasia: Opposing Viewpoints.* San Diego: Greenhaven, 2002.

Elizabeth Atwood Gailey — *Write to Death: New Framing of the Right to Die Conflict, from Quinlan's Coma to Kevorkian's Conviction.* Westport, CT: Praeger, 2003.

James Haley, ed. — *Death and Dying: Opposing Viewpoints.* San Diego: Greenhaven, 2003.

Derek Humphrey — *Final Exit: The Practicalities of Self-Deliverance and Assisted Suicide for the Dying.* New York: Dell, 2002.

Derek Humphrey — *The Good Euthanasia Guide 2004: Where, What, and Who in Choices in Dying.* Junction City, OR: Norris Lane, 2004.

Derek Humphrey — *Lawful Exit: The Limits of Freedom for Help in Dying.* Collingdale, PA: DIANE, 2001.

Roger S. Magnusson — *Angels of Death: Exploring the Euthanasia Underground.* New Haven, CT: Yale University Press, 2002.

Barbara A. Olevitch — *Protecting Psychiatric Patients and Others from the Assisted-Suicide Movement: Insights and Strategies.* Westport, CT: Praeger, 2002.

M. Scott Peck — *Denial of the Soul: Spiritual and Medical Perspectives on Euthanasia.* New York: Crown, 1998.

Timothy E. Quill and Margaret P. Battin, eds. — *Physician-Assisted Dying: The Case for Palliative Care and Patient Choice.* Baltimore: Johns Hopkins University Press, 2004.

Barry Rosenfeld — *Assisted Suicide and the Right to Die: The Interface of Social Science, Public Policy, and Medical Ethics.* Washington, DC: American Psychological Association, 2004.

87

88

Jennifer M. Scherer and Rita J. Simon — *Euthanasia and the Right to Die: A Comparative View*. Lanham, MD: Rowman & Littlefield, 1999.

J. Donald Smith — *Right-to-Die Policies in the American States: Judicial and Legislative Innovation*. New York: LFB Scholarly Publishing, 2002.

Margaret Somerville — *Death Talk: The Case Against Euthanasia and Physician-Assisted Suicide*. Montreal: McGill-Queen's University Press, 2001.

Robert F. Weir — *Abating Treatment with Critically Ill Patients: Ethical and Legal Limits to the Medical Prolongation of Life*. Oxford: Oxford University Press, 1990.

Sue Woodman — *Last Rights: The Struggle over the Right to Die*. New York: Perseus, 2001.

Periodicals

Daniel Avila — "Assisted Suicide and the Inalienable Right to Life," *Issues in Law & Medicine*, Fall 2000.

Robert Barry — "The Papal Allocution on Caring for Persons in a 'Vegetative State,'" *Issues in Law & Medicine*, Fall 2004.

Susan Bell — "Euthanasia—a Wish or Workable Reality?" *Cancer Nursing Practice*, October 2003.

Arian Campo-Flores — "Who Has the Right to Die?" *Newsweek*, November 3, 2003.

Gerald D. Coleman — "Take and Eat: Morality and Medically Assisted Feeding," *America*, April 5, 2004.

Licia Corbella — "Right to Die Turns into Duty," October 3, 2004. www.canoe.ca.

Michael Coren — "Never Say Die, or Right to Die," December 18, 2004. www.canoe.ca.

Beth Dalbey — "Pets and People Deserve to Die with Grace, Dignity," *Business Record*, January 28, 2002.

Alison Davis — "Living with Dignity," *Observer*, November 10, 2002.

Len Doyal and Lesley Doyal — "Why Active Euthanasia and Physician-Assisted Suicide Should Be Legalized," *British Medical Journal*, November 10, 2001.

Daniel Eisenberg — "Lessons of the Schiavo Battle: What the Bitter Fight over a Woman's Right to Live or Die Tells Us About Politics, Religion, the Courts, and Life Itself," *Time*, April 4, 2005.

Bobbie Farsides and Robert J. Dunlop — "Is There Such a Thing as a Life Not Worth Living?" *British Medical Journal*, June 16, 2001.

Carol Bernstein Ferry — "A Good Death," *Nation*, September 17, 2001.

Joyce S. Fontana	"Rational Suicide in the Terminally Ill," *Journal of Nursing Scholarship*, Summer 2002.
Faye Girsh	"How Shall We Die?" *Free Inquiry*, Winter 2001.
Pamela Hennessy	"The Means to an End—Terri Schiavo and the Right to Die," May 11, 2004. www.opinion editorials.com.
Nat Hentoff	"Terri Schiavo: Judicial Murder," *San Diego Union-Tribune*, April 3, 2005.
John Paul II	"Life-Sustaining Treatments in a Vegetative State," *Issues in Law & Medicine*, Fall 2004.
John F. Kavanaugh	"Food for Terri Schiavo," *America*, November 24, 2003.
Garret Keizer	"Life Everlasting: The Religious Right and the Right to Die," *Harper's Magazine*, February 2005.
Daniel E. Lee	"Physician-Assisted Suicide: A Conservative Critique of Intervention," *Hastings Center Report*, January/February 2003.
Ruth Macklin	"Dignity Is a Useless Concept: It Means No More than Respect for Persons or Their Autonomy," *British Medical Journal*, December 20, 2003.
Ken MacQueen	"Choosing Suicide: Right-to-Die Activists Are Fighting New Battles," *Maclean's*, August 5, 2002.
K. L. Marsala	"For the Sake of Terri Schiavo," *American Thinker*, March 10, 2005.
Kathryn E. Mazzeo	"The Right to Die Versus the Right to Live, Who Decides? The Long and Wandering Road to a Legislative Solution," *Albany Law Review*, Fall 2002.
David McKenzie	"Church, State, and Physician-Assisted Suicide," *Journal of Church and State*, Autumn 2004.
Robert D. Orr	"Ethics and Life's Ending: An Exchange," *First Things*, August/September 2004.
Anna Quindlen	"The Culture of Each Life," *Newsweek*, April 4, 2005.
Cindy Richards	"Opting for Death with Dignity," *Chicago Sun-Times*, March 30, 2005.
Margot Roosevelt	"Choosing Their Time: The Next Contentious End-of-life Issue: Assisted Suicide," *Time*, April 4, 2005.
Debra J. Saunders	"Death Trumps Choice," *San Francisco Chronicle*, January 6, 2005.
Debra J. Saunders	"Death with Vanity," *San Francisco Chronicle*, January 4, 2005.
Teresa A. Savage	"An Argument Against Mercy Killing," *Pediatric Nursing*, July/August 2003.

Jeffrey A. Schaler	"Living and Dying the State's Way," *Liberty*, August 2003.
Carl E. Schneider	"All My Rights," *Hastings Center Report*, July/August 2002.
Peter Singer	"Freedom and the Right to Die," *Free Inquiry*, Spring 2002.
Peter Singer	"Ms. B. and Diane Pretty: A Commentary," *Journal of Medical Ethics*, August 2002.
Wesley J. Smith	"Taking Requests, Doing Harm," *Human Life Review*, Summer 2003.
Wesley J. Smith	"Why Secular Humanism Is Wrong About Assisted Suicide," *Free Inquiry*, Spring 2003.
Keith Taylor	"Was Dr. Kevorkian Right?" *Free Inquiry*, Spring 2003.
Ingrid Tischer	"No Guts, No Glory: Where Are the Feminists on Terri Schiavo?" *Off Our Backs*, January/February 2004.
Ja Emerson Vermaat	"Euthanasia in the Third Reich: Lessons for Today?" *Issues in Law & Medicine*, Summer 2002.

Index